EVERY SON,

A **JOSEPH**

IN THE MAKING

Learning from the hero who made it
Genesis 37 – 50

Rev. Paul Ekal Lokol

Foreword by

DR. KENNEDY KIMUTAI KIRUI

Every Son, a Joseph in the Making

DEDICATION

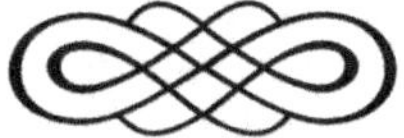

I dedicate this book to my sons –
Ewen, Joseph, and Jabez. Be the Josephs' of today.

ACKNOWLEDGMENT

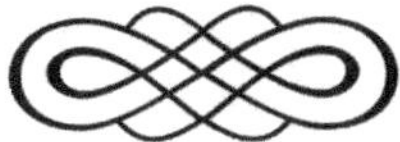

I sincerely thank my heavenly father for His gracious hand upon me to complete this book. The burning desire to share God's blessings with me in the written format has given me greater joy than ever.

Thanks to my lovely wife, Joyce Akai, and our beautiful young ones – Dianne, Ewen, Joseph, Abigail, and Jabez for your patience and moral support in developing this great piece. You have been a great family, and I forever cherish your love and care for our time together in this life and the years to come. You are special.

To my editors, you helped me bring my thoughts harmoniously and diligently. You guys enabled me to share my inspirational tale message on Joseph. In addition, you have been so helpful and gracious in your comments and extra-mile support.

Dr. Kennedy Kirui, you have become my senior brother in my life and academic journey. Your mentorship, moral support, and life journeys together have been instrumental in my writing life. Your writing genius has encouraged me to keep up the fire. Thank you so much, my brother. You mean a lot to me.

Mr. Shem Tangus. You have been a great leader and a friend indeed. Since I joined Tenwek Hospital in my current capacity, you have not stopped encouraging, guiding, challenging, and correcting me in love. This book has come out within this time; you have been my boss and friend. You are a good leader and a great mentor. It has been an honor to serve under your leadership.

TABLE OF CONTENTS

FOREWORD

I have known Paul for more than two decades, and during that time, I have seen tremendous growth in his life as an administrator, teacher, scholar, husband, and father. Yet, despite the growth, change of roles, and workstations, he has consistently demonstrated an undying commitment and devotion to God, which reflects in all aspects of his life; He is a godly man. He is a man of integrity. He epitomizes resilience and determination and allows his environment and life's challenges to influence his destiny. He continuously demonstrates courage and determination to be where God wants him to be and to do what God wants him to do.

In this new book, which I highly recommend, Paul reminds us that everyone wants to live for something significant and for their lives to count for something greater than themselves. He has written a fantastic book, skillfully integrating scripture and intersecting that with his life story to help you from scripture and experience to live a life of significance and impact. Therefore, I highly recommend this book by my dear friend to anyone who desires a life of meaning.

Paul, carefully tracing Joseph's life journey and experiences, highlights the steps we should take as we navigate the different phases and shifts of life in God's favor. He will help you understand God's purpose for your life and what you must do to enjoy the grace of God, irrespective of what life throws your way. The challenge with most people is not daring to dream but not knowing how to harness their God-given dreams. Using Joseph's story, the author helps you understand that the foundation of living a life of significance and meaning is honoring God in every aspect.

Many people collapse under the weight of their success because they are unprepared for it. Paul helps you avoid this by providing biblical principles to address the allurement of power, pleasure, and prestige. Irrespective of our placement and positions in life, whether at the palace or prison, as a leader or servant, young or old, we can live a life of honor by not giving in to compromise, complacency, and compliance to sin or world systems.

Many want to be different, but few want to change. This book reminds us that there is no shortcut to success. Trust the process. No pain, no gain. No cross, no crown. Be willing to pay the price. God does not waste any experience; it all works for good. The call to a life of significance and impact is a call to be different. Dare to be different; dare to be a Joseph in your generation.

Dr. Kennedy Kimutai Kirui
Founder and Executive Director for University Discipleship Movement and the Lead Pastor at United Faith Chapel, Kampala – Uganda.

INTRODUCTION

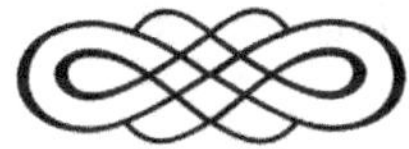

Joseph was the son of the patriarch Jacob and his wife, Rachel. As Jacob's name became synonymous with all of Israel, Joseph was eventually equated with all the tribes that made up the northern kingdom. According to tradition, his bones were buried at Shechem, the oldest shrines of the north (Joshua 24:32). Joseph's story is told in Genesis 37 - 50. It is the complete package of any son in a real family and a balanced view of life.

Joseph, the most beloved of Jacob's sons, is hated by his envious brothers. Angry and jealous of Jacob's gift to Joseph, a splendid "coat of many colors," the brothers seize him and sell him to a party of Ishmaelites, or Midianites, who carry him to Egypt. There, Joseph eventually gains the favor of the pharaoh of Egypt through his interpretation of a dream and obtains a high place in the pharaoh's kingdom. His acquisition of grain supplies enabled Egypt to withstand a famine. Driven by the same famine, his brothers journeyed from Canaan to Egypt to obtain food. They prostrated themselves before Joseph, but they could not recognize him. After Joseph reconciled with his brothers, he invited Jacob's whole household to come to Goshen in Egypt, where a settlement was provided for the family and their flocks. His brothers' selling Joseph into slavery proved providential in the end — since it protected the family from famine. The family's descendants grew and multiplied into the Hebrew nation, eventually departing from Egypt for Israel.

The story of Joseph often called a novella, is a carefully wrought piece of literary craftsmanship. Though it features the personality of Joseph, it is introduced (Genesis 37:2) as the "history of the family of Jacob." Scholars agree that parts of the story show dependence upon the ancient Egyptian "Tale of Two Brothers," but in characteristically Hebraic fashion, the narrator in Genesis has ignored the mythical and magical motifs in the Egyptian tale, and the focus of the outcome is placed on its meaning for the whole house of Israel.

In this book, we'll understand the careful steps we must take to live like Joseph, who made heaven open for him in all ramifications of life. We'll understand the purpose of God for our lives and what must be done to enjoy the grace of God for eternity. Every son who wants to emulate the life of Joseph must keep harnessing their God-given dreams, keep themselves away from sin, run from temptations, work hard, be prayerful, be holy, fear the Lord, be positive, and always be ready to work and serve God.

Joseph's position changed from a beloved son to an enslaved person, then to a prisoner, and finally to a ruler, and God was always with him. God, too, can be with you if only you can learn the secrets from this son – Joseph. Enjoy the reading!

Remain blessed,
Rev. Paul Ekal Lokol

Chapter 1

JOSEPH'S PATHWAY TO DESTINY

Genesis 37: 1 – 14

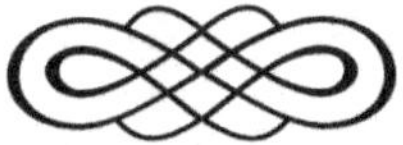

Destiny is no matter of chance. It is a matter of choice.
It is not a thing to be waited for; it is a thing to be achieved.
William Jennings Bryan

You will agree that it takes a lot to create or produce anything new; reproducing isn't also accessible. Every good product you see out there goes through the making process. Everyone likes the end product of gold, diamond, silver, and a few other refined mineral resources, but if we can see some of these products in their raw states, we would prefer something else.

These products inevitably go through FIRE in their making process. It takes fire to bring out the beauty in them. The fire helps in removing the impurities in them and also helps in shaping them. In some cases, the fire will heap these products to the extent that they will melt off completely; but you know what? The liquid product will be cast into another mold to give it a new shape. Note that the old has to offer a way to a unique body type. God is working on a man like me and you; He sometimes wounds and chisels you to shape. As a young man growing up, you may wonder what this life has for me. Although I have been a young man like you for an entire time, the far that I have reached is enough to tell me that there is gold in this life that I need to discover daily. The reason is that there is much in store for me as a son of God. Mine is to confirm to you as we delve into this first chapter that we all need the making to be what God wants of us. Learn the secrets of this beautiful adventure we have just started.

People easily name their children Joseph, not for the meaning but for the reputation of that character in the bible. Some even give themselves the name, thinking they will automatically assume the character. Yet, you read headline news, see some apprehended armed robbers bearing the name Joseph, and wonder if it is an accurate presentation of Joseph we know in the bible. So many p there want to be like Joseph, but are they ready to go through what Joseph went through?

In this chapter, we shall look at how Joseph rose from nothing to something, how he came out of the pit and got sold out, and how he eventually rose to become a prominent figure even in a foreign land. The truth is, this chapter is very vital to where we are going in this book. It is foundational at the core. All that Joseph did later on has a direct connection to this beginning.

Let's examine how the making process began.

Get Busy with Something

*"These are the generations of Jacob. **At seventeen years old, Joseph was feeding the flock with his brethren; the lad was with the sons of Bilhah, and with the sons of Zilpah, his Father's wives: Joseph brought them** unto his Father their evil report."* Gen 37:2

The highlighted portion is of utmost interest in this verse. The scriptures rightly captured that Joseph fed his Father's flock with his brothers. He was only 17 at this point, which is interesting. He wasn't around in the name "daddy's boy"; OK, daddy seems to have a soft spot for him, but was it really for no reason? I don't think so! Jacob loved Joseph because of Rachel, agreed! But he also loved him because he feared God. We'll see more about that later on.

Note that at this juncture, Joseph hadn't dreamt. He hadn't found purpose yet. Joseph was just a young boy with plenty of elder brothers, possibly trying to learn from the seniors but finding none worthy of emulation. But Joseph never sat idle in the house like Jacob would've loved; he found a way to join his brothers on the farm to feed the animals.

The point is, before finding purpose, you must be busy. Get busy if you desire to see your life's and destiny's vision. Let's take a look at these two scriptures:

"Whatsoever your hand finds to do, do it heartily; as unto the Lord, and not as unto men." Colossians 3:23

For those in the transition period of school, especially In-between your high school and college/University, don't just sit at home watching films; move from one season film to another. Lay your hands on something; try to learn a skill, especially digital skills. Enroll in a course, and keep learning. Keep adding value to yourself;

this will better position you for opportunities. In 2007, I was teaching at AGC Lokichar secondary school. I registered for my Post Graduate Diploma in Education (PGDE) to help me teach better in that High school. However, after two years, I left teaching and became an administrator with the government of Kenya. On my side, I thought about that Diploma, which seemed like a waste of money. I felt terrible about it but did not have anything to say because I was ashamed of my decision. In 2019, my denomination asked me to head Tenwek Hospital College – School of chaplaincy. During this period, I did not know what was ahead of me. One of my assignments was registering for the college immediately, spearheading the formulation of the chaplaincy curriculum with the Republic of Kenya. Little did I know that as soon as the college was registered and we started administering a government-approved curriculum, the head of that institution was required to have done pedagogy or trained as a teacher. You know what? I laughed at myself when I remembered the moments back in 20en I hated myself for doing that PGDE. It was God's awaited moment. There is an opportune time for it. Our God does not waste anything we do or go through.

"Whatsoever thy hand finds to do, do it with thy might; for there is no work, device, knowledge, or whoever in the grave, whither thou goes." Ecclesiastes 9:10

God does not use lazy people. From Genesis to Revelation, everyone God has ever used was not lazy; God created man to care for the garden in the first place; He specifically commanded Adam to take care of the garden. Elisha was right on the farm when he got the call of God, Moses was busy with the sheep when he got the call, Peter was on the sea when he got the call, Matthew was right in his office when Jesus called him, and the sons of Zebedee were also busy with their Father when Jesus called them. It would be best if you were active in discovering your purpose.

So cheer up just as Joseph cared for his Father's flock; it was easy for him to do it well in Potiphar's house. Anything you do or learn now will play a role in your life tomorrow. Are you busy with something significant? If you do, you won't have time for youthful lust and other social vices; you will abstain from evil.

Abstain from Evil

*"These are the generations of Jacob. At seventeen years old, Joseph was feeding the flock with his brethren; the lad was with the sons of Bilhah, and with the sons of Zilpah, his Father's wives: Joseph brought them **unto his Father their evil report.**"*

Gen 37:2

"And have no fellowship with the unfruitful works of darkness, but rather expose them." Ephesians 5:11

Of the significant challenges of the young ones of this generation is an inability to abstain from sin and its elements. Yet, abstinence has diminished drastically, especially in the last few decades. Why is it so? Well, it's in fulfillment of the scriptures. Jesus said, "Iniquities shall increase, and the love of many shall wax cold" (Matthew 24:12).

Douglas, a sixteen aged guy, shared his experience on how he became a drug addict in a boarding school and eventually became a notorious boy who was known for his drug addiction guy until the light of God shone on his way. Douglas was brilliant and easygoing; he always came either first or second in the class. His teachers loved him, and his parents and everyone around him loved him. When other students had issues with any subject that had to do with calculations, Mathematics, Physics, Chemistry, and the like, they would go to him for assistance. To tell you how brilliant he was, he was a science student who never attended any commercial class but would help commercial students solve problems on Financial Accounts; can you imagine the kind of brain he possessed?

A few of Douglas's friends, Malik and Peter, were secret smokers of all substances. Peter's parents were eminent people in society and had so much money. So he would compel his driver to supply the drugs discretely. The school needed to discover this quickly because they would wrap among his provisions and other chops.

After a while, Peter decided to introduce Douglas to it; Douglas was initially reluctant but gave in after a while. The reason was that Peter had been eating snacks during break time since he got into that school. In addition, Douglas's parents needed more money. The truth is, Douglas had the option of saying no to losing break time allowance from Peter, but he instead decided to compromise his stand on smoking weed and other complex substances. So instead of reporting them, unlike Joseph, he joined them.

In the case of Joseph, he not only refused to do what the brothers were doing but fulfilled the scriptures by exposing them (Eph 5:11). Joseph was in an evil-characterized environment. His brothers would probably be engaged in serious crimes of the time, but Joseph stood out. Have you ever fought sin with all sincerity? You recall that the oil of gladness and the supernatural came on Jesus because He hated iniquity and loved righteousness (Heb 1:9). You must be deliberate about avoiding all forms of sinful indulgence. The book of Proverbs advises us not to consent to sinners if they attempt to entice us. Take to your heels. Be a saint in Sodom. Serve God in Babylon. God is counting on you!

Expose Evil

Any great catalyst to the making of a man is the ability to reprove and expose evil. Joseph always told his Father of the ills committed by his brothers whenever they returned home from the farm. Joseph couldn't rebuke or challenge his brothers for doing evil because he was younger than them; he had to apply wisdom to avoid issues with them. So he resorted to telling his Father what they did wrong on the field. What do you think the Father would do in this case? He would love Joseph the more.

Every parent loves a well-behaved child. But Jacob's love for Joseph was more than being Rachel's son. Joseph earned his Father's love through his actions and attitude. So, how do you behave at home? Can your parents trust you with your own life or anything in that home, or are you the bad one in the house who is associated with anything going wrong at any given time?

If you desire God's direction and Presence in your life, you must learn to shine the light of Christ wherever you find yourself. Overcome the darkness around you and not the other way around. Let people see you and try to hide because they are in the wrong place. Be bold to identify with Jesus everywhere you go; don't try to hide the fact that you're a Christian. Let your light so shine before men that they may see your good works and glorify God through you.

Whenever God sees a man or woman, boy or girl, who is ready and determined to expose evil and embrace righteousness, God singles out such for an unprecedented and viable destiny. God begins to show them clues pointing to where they are going. Such a person must have sharpened their spiritual sense organs over time. Their ability to receive is enhanced; no network glitches, and there's a deep flow from God to them. The truth is that abstinence from evil builds intimacy with God.

What happened to Joseph next? Let's find out!

Be Visionary and Purposeful

Another defining factor and catalyst in the making of Joseph was his ability to see the future from then. He was visionary and purposeful. Yes, he had all cleared, and there were no sin barricades, no glitches, and he could hear God. Let us have a look at the scriptures:

"And Joseph dreamed a dream, and he told it to his brethren: and they hated him more. And he said unto them, Hear, I pray you, this dream which I have dreamed: for, behold, we were binding sheaves in the field, and, lo, my sheaf arose, and also stood upright; and, behold, your sheaves stood round about, and made obeisance to my sheaf. And his brethren said to him, Shalt thou indeed reign over us? Or shalt thou indeed have dominion over us? And they hated him yet the more for his dreams and his words."

Genesis 37:5-8

Joseph had a dream, and he told his brothers about it. Now, one question I always ask myself is that why Joseph? Why not Reuben of any of the senior sons of Jacob? Why does it have to be Joseph? Of course, we all are entitled to dream, and we all have dreams; but why was it that Joseph was the only one dreaming?

By dreaming, we do not mean sleeping with numerous activities in mind. You know that some of us desire multiple things in our minds. Joseph's dreams were revelations and not mere dreams. He was catching the vision of his life and destiny. Brill summarizes Joseph's dream very well when he says, "Three things are foreshadowed: 1. Joseph will one day enjoy an exalted status over his family, 2. his brothers will come to do obeisance, and 3. his father and mother will later do the same."[1] His eyes were opened to see what the future held for him. Remember, he was busy, stayed away from evil, and exposed corruption when he could. His relationship with God had grown over time; he had a very intimate fellowship with the Spirit of God. Hence, he understood God when He spoke to him.

This is unlike many of us (young ones) today; instead of standing out to receive from God, we join the multitude to do evil. The grip of pornographic movies has robbed us of the ability to decipher the language of the Spirit, masturbation won't let us catch the vision for tomorrow, and premarital sex and pleasures of life hold us from taking advantage of God's illuminating light.

At age seventeen, Joseph was already catching the vision of God for his life; what an early way to discover your purpose! Can there be a better time? Some of us at this time have experimented with all manner of evils, like trying out a first kiss, smoking a cigarette, and other terrible things. Joseph was so focused on the future that he had no time for today's youthful sinful pleasures. Joseph was upgrading his life physically and spiritually to have no space for anything else. Isn't that exemplary? You're 18, 20, or even 25 years

---

[1] Leiden E.J. Brill, *A Study of the Biblical Story of Joseph (Genesis 37 - 50)*, vol. XX (Netherlands, 1970), 1.

old; what vision do you have? At 17 years old, Joseph caught his eye; how positioned are you to start seeing your tomorrow from today?

Keep Dreaming

"And he dreamed yet another dream, and told it his brethren, and said, behold, I have dreamed a dream more; and, behold, the sun and the moon and the eleven stars made obeisance to me. And he told it to his Father, and his brethren: and his Father rebuked him, and said unto him, what is this dream that thou hast dreamed? Shall I and thy mother and thy brethren indeed come to bow down ourselves to thee to the earth?"

Genesis 37:9-10

One of the beautiful things I learned about Joseph's dreams in my readings on the Amazing facts international website was that Joseph was ironically nicknamed *'ba'al hakhalomot*, which meant the 'dreamer' according to Genesis 37:19. Which implied 'master of dreams.' It continues that "this title fits him very well because he not only receives, understands, and interprets prophetic dreams, but also fulfills them in his life."[2] To fulfill your purpose, you consistently know what God demands of your season. If the last time you had a solid revelation that pointed to the direction of your destiny was a year ago, you need to do better; and seek help as soon as possible. You m becons consistently receive instructions from God; this enhances the speed of accomplishment. If God tells you

---

[2] Amazing Facts International, "Devotional: Joseph, Master of Dreams: Lesson 11," June 11, 2022, accessed February 4, 2023, https://www.amazingfacts.org/media-library/media/e/26730/t/joseph--master-of-dreams.

this is your destiny, He has much more to unveil to you in due course. You must seek to know more about it to aid clarity.

Please look at Joseph's first dream; it slightly differed from the second one. The inclusion of the sun and the moon makes it more profound than what he had in the first dream. Joseph needed a second dream to understand his destiny better. Even his sibling and parents got the meaning of the dream and got worried about what the outcome could be.

Another thing I would like you to know is that Joseph had an intimate relationship with God. The dreams attest to his commitment to doing the will of the Father. Therefore, you must be hungry to see and achieve more for God and yourself. If God has helped you achieve something today, press hard to get direction for the following line of action. Don't ever relax and become complacent.

You must do everything possible to keep dreaming and hearing from God because what you see is what you get. The fundamental determinant of fulfilling destiny is the ability to see and perceive. Your spiritual foresight defines your entire existence. The height you attain is directly proportional to how well you see. What can you see? I remember back in 2008 when I was in form 3. I was suspended for one year from school because of praying at night. Praying at night had been prohibited by the school administration because of the school's religious orientation. It took the hand of God through my pastor for me to return to school. During that absence from school, I did receive sought of a dream to serve God in full-time ministry. This made me focus on what I was looking for in life. I committed to further this dream by completing school and joining theological training to serve the Lord better. Even though the University Joint Admission Board selected me to join the Bachelor of Science at the Chepkoilel campus of Moi University, I went ahead. I pursued a degree in theology at Kenya Highlands Bible college. I have not regretted following that dream from that tiny beginning. Do not despise the days of those initial dreams. God has a way of expanding and following our goals with more details and continues to unfold them one at a time.

Parental Observation

Parenting today has taken an entirely different shape, different from what was obtainable in the days of our forefathers; however, certain parenting principles are universal across generations. Let's take a look at what Jacob did with Joseph's dreams.

"And his brethren envied him, **but his father observed the saying."**

Genesis 37:11

Jacob also played a significant role in the making of Joseph. The scripture we read above shows that Jacob brooded over Joseph's dreams; he must have tried to tailor his life in the direction of his dreams. No doubt, the dreams gave Jacob a clue about what would become of Joseph; he probably had made sure Joseph did things right in the light of the will of God and His commandments.

Mary, the mother of Jesus, did almost exactly what Jacob did. Take a look at what Luke 2:19 says;

"But Mary treasured up all these things and pondered them in her heart" *(NIV)*

Can you see that? Mary kept what the angel told her about the destiny of Jesus and pondered on them. She took time to reflect on them. No wonder she understood her son very well even when others seemed not to. That was why she boldly met Jesus at the marriage ceremony in Canaan when there was no wine and told His disciples, "Whatever He asks you to do, go ahead and do it."

The parental role in helping a child become what God wants them to be is crucial. Every parent must come to this understanding. But first, they must try to understand what God wants for their children and what they want for them. So, parents should labor in prayers to understand the will of God for their children; and allow God to do with their children what He dims fit for their lives. They need to know that they should not be obstacles to what God wants to do in their children's lives; instead, they need to support them in the best way possible.

Absolute Obedience

One more critical factor in the making of Joseph was his obedience to his Father's instructions. He wasn't disobedient to his parents. Let's take a look at the verse below;

*"And Israel said unto Joseph, do not thy brethren feed the flock in Shechem? Come, and I will send thee unto them. And he said to him, **"Here am I."** And he said to him, go, I pray thee, see whether it be well with thy brethren and the flocks, and bring me word again. So, he sent him out of the vale of Hebron, and he came to Shechem.* Genesis 37:13-14

The highlighted phrase in the passage depicts total obedience; **"Here Am I"**! Heaven is always happy whenever it sees a yielded vessel here on earth. Prophet Isaiah also showed this level of surrender to God when he told God in Isaiah 6:8, "…. Here I am. Send me!" If you are too full of yourself, if your people can't talk to you, and you obey, you may not go far in life's journey. Many of us are disobedient to our parents; when they speak to us, we don't want to listen to them. Our school teachers can correct us; even our Sunday school teachers in the church can't talk to some of us, yet we want to rise to the top like Joseph. Beloved, God isn't a joker. The matters of destiny are serious ones. No one becomes great by mere wishes; no one becomes relevant to their society without being mindful of each of the catalysts discussed above.

When God sees a heart that obeys, He goes the extra mile to manifest Himself through such a person. We must therefore learn to humble ourselves before our earthly leaders and before God so He can use us. Obey God anyhow!

Chapter 2

JOSEPH FACED DESTINY HUNTERS

Genesis 37: 5 – 36

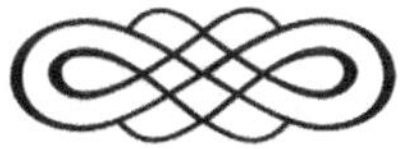

Dreams can either die young or mature to become realities, depending on how they are handled! — **Israelmore Ayivor, Shaping the dream**

God has a pattern for dealing with men, especially those with enviable destinies. Have you ever asked yourself why every great person you've seen has terrible stories to tell? Someone said, "Behind every glory is a story."[3] It is even more pathetic when it comes to those whom God uses to change the narrative in a home, family, community, state, country, continent, or globe. The truth is, your assignment in life defines your path or route.

Typical of a human being, you feel happy when you can see where you're going; there's a good vision, clarity, and direction. But sometimes, we are often caught unaware by the wind of self-deception. We either unveil the vision too early or jump into action without asking God for strength, wisdom, and "how" to actualize the vision. As a result, we often fall into this pit and spend more than the average time fulfilling our mandate here on earth.

Every good destiny attracts both good and bad. The good will come hoping to tap from your future, but the bad will come looking for a way to halt or truncate your destiny. Isn't that wickedness? Now, it becomes more dangerous when the enemies of your future are members of your household. I feel the anguish of King David when he said;

"For it was not an enemy that reproached me; then I could have borne it: neither was it he that hated me that did magnify himself against me; then I would have hid from him: **but it was thou, a man mine equal, my guide, and my acquaintance. So we took sweet counsel and walked to God's house in a company."**

Psalms 55:12-14

---

[3] Brenda Calvine, "Behind Every Glory There a Is a Story," *Behind Every Glory There Is a Story*, 2015, http://brendacalvince.blogspot.com/2015/01/behind-every-glory-there-is-story.html.

If it is an outside enemy, I would've known what to do; but it is you, my acquaintance, my very friend, and my family member. Therefore, this section is also crucial, as we shall touch deep into these areas with real-life lessons from them.

Is it Bad to Share my Dreams?

It's natural to want to share a dream with someone, but how you do it is what matters. For Joseph as a teenager, he shared his vision with excitement without knowing it could cause him something. He was just an innocent young man trying to do his best to share the best he had with his brother. But, no! It was simply a display of ignorance and lack of information management.

Let's examine that verse again.

"And Joseph dreamed a dream, and he told it to his brethren: *and they hated him more. And he said unto them, hear, I pray you, this dream which I have dreamed: for, behold, we were binding sheaves in the field, and, lo, my sheaf arose, and also stood upright; and, behold, your sheaves stood round about, and made obeisance to my sheaf. And his brethren said to him, shall thou indeed reign over us? Or shall thou indeed have dominion over us? And they hated him yet the more for his dreams and his words."*

Genesis 37:5-8

As much as you would say Joseph was ignorant of what he was doing, he could have managed the divine information better. Some also argue that Prophet Habakkuk told us that we should write the vision and make it public so we can run fast with it Habakkuk 2:2. It's a fact that every image should be written down or documented for easy analysis and accountability.

One thing you must know is that there are revelations that are for your knowledge and consumption. And every revelation has its timing regarding sharing, daring, and fulfillment. Sometimes you need to verify by asking God for clarity, praying, do some underground spiritual digging before sharing your vision. It's okay to share your dream, but you must be careful how you share your vision with people. So, don't be too hasty to let the cat out of the bag.

We live in a world full of jealousy, envy, and all forms of evil, especially in what you reveal to people about yourself. So if Joseph's brothers could work against his dreams, how much more an outsider? The reason is that good destinies attract both good and bad.

Good Dreams Attracts both Good and Bad

"And Joseph dreamed a dream, and he told it his brethren: and they hated him yet the more." Genesis 37:5

"And his brethren envied him, but his father observed the saying." Genesis 37:11

Envy is a universal occurrence; when you present a better proposal than your colleagues at the workplace, they often hate you for it. If you keep coming first in school or sports among your peers, some will love you, while others will hate you.

Mind you, if your rising attempts to displace someone to assume their position, be ready for severe opposition and resistance. It also happened to Joseph. It was apparent that Joseph was going to rise above them all. It was a good dream, the vision was clear enough that everyone who listened to it got the meaning without stress, but they were limited in their understanding of what God was going to do with the life of Joseph. However, on the surface, they knew he would be greater than them; what immediately came to their mind was family hierarchy and inheritance. They had put one and two together to try to understand what would become of Joseph. They asked themselves, "Is this guy going to be the heir to our father's wealth? Will he rule this home one day while we bow to him?" As much as their thinking wasn't entirely out of place, they got it wrong; God was cooking something else. The bottom line is that you must be careful sharing your dreams. Ask for wisdom in dealing with your elders as your life unveils in phases. God will show us mercy and will not allow satanic plots against our destinies to destroy us in Jesus' name!

The Plot Against Destiny

I explained earlier that every great destiny attracts both good and bad. The bad sometimes go the extra mile trying to undo the greatness of the future. In the case of Joseph, there was a plot against his dream. It looked like the plot was against his life on the surface, but the truth is that they were particular about fulfilling his dreams. Hence, they said, "…. let us see what will become of his dreams…."

If you're genuinely born again, redeemed by the blood of Jesus, saved by the power of the sacrifice on the cross, and washed by His precious blood, know that you've signed up for an extraordinary destiny, and the devil will be after you. Let's see how they plotted against Joseph.

"And when they saw him afar off, even before he came near them, **they conspired against him to slay him.** *And they said one to another, behold, this dreamer cometh.* **Come now, and let us slay him, kill him**

into some pit, and we will say some evil beast hath devoured him: **and we shall see what will become of his dreams.** "

Genesis 37:18-20

People often say, "I don't just know why these people are against me; what have I done? Why are they after me?" Please permit me to digress a little to drive a point home. Have you noticed that some people can go to any length to retain their relevance, even if they have to kill? The sought relevance happens virtually in all settings, including so-called houses of worship. Some unfortunate men have given themselves to this, forgetting that God promotes or demotes. The psalmist says, He sets down one and sets up another. Who can question God's authority?

The brothers of Joseph conspired against him; to do what? To kill him! If I may ask, kill him for what? They conspired to kill him because he was a dreamer. Should you kill someone because they have dreams to fulfill? Should you work against someone because you can see greatness ahead of him? Should you stylishly plot the downfall of someone because he would rise above you someday?

Envy, sadly, is the reality of the society in which we live. The brothers of Joseph were his leaders by family hierarchy, just like some are bosses over a couple of people in our offices, and some of us are leaders even in God's house over other young believers. So, what do you do when you notice a special grace upon someone under you, especially when it is a global assignment? Do you wholeheartedly encourage and assist such a person in growing, or do you find a way to tame it for selfish reasons?

This is one reason the dreamer must possess the spiritual intelligence to deal with those ahead of us. If you are a young person with great dreams, be extremely careful how you deal with the elderly ones in the same field as you. There will always be a plot somewhere against anyone relevant to God and society at large.

The last statement in the passage above is something you mustn't miss in this segment. **"....and we shall see what will become of his dreams"**. The plot was actually against destiny and not his body. I imagine them saying, "Let's make sure he doesn't overtake us, let's make sure he doesn't take our place, let's make sure he doesn't become the crowned prince of the kingdom of Jacob...... They wanted to ensure he didn't become what he had seen. I stand to pray for every young one who will have the opportunity to read this book; the devil will not truncate your destiny in Jesus's name. Every satanic agent in human form, plotting against the fulfillment of your dreams and visions, I declare that their plans will not stand in the name of Jesus. Amen!

Destiny is preserved through Reuben's Intervention.

Whenever the enemy plans for evil, God is always there to thwart his effort. For example, Joseph's brothers plotted, but God spoke through Rueben to stop them from killing him. Do you know why? God needed him to stay alive to fulfill his divine mandate. No wonder the Bible says, "Behold, they shall surely gather together, but not by me: whosoever shall gather together against thee shall fall for thy sake" (Isaiah 54:15). There is nothing you can do to stop a bird from flying over your head. Still, there's everything you can do to prevent a bird from making a nest on your head.

God used Reuben to confuse the enemy on the spot.

*"**And Reuben heard it, delivered him out of their hands,** and said, Let us not kill him. And Reuben said unto them, shed no*

blood, but cast him into this pit in the wilderness, and lay no hand upon him; he might rid him of their hands, to deliver him to his father again."

Genesis 37:21-22

"And Reuben heard it and delivered him out of their hands…." What do you see here? For me, I see God in action. At this juncture, I hear heaven react to the plot to kill him; I imagine God says, what! Do you want to kill a generational deliverer? Do you want to kill my plans to preserve my elect? Do you want to destroy my plans to sustain Israel forever? No way! God immediately spoke through Reuben. That's God for you. But guess what; did God ultimately save Joseph from trouble? Not at all! Do you know what? The experiences were part of God's plan to land Joseph on the throne. But one thing that isn't part of the plan is death. So, God stepped in quickly to cancel that, ensuring the devil did not hijack the process.

Destiny was reserved again through Judah's Intervention.

However, Judah's intervention was needed to transport Joseph to his next school, or destiny. God will always preserve your dream every step of the way. God will never stop to protect His own. He said He would never leave us nor forsake us. No matter the plot, He will always show up for us. So God showed up again for Joseph.

"And Judah said unto his brethren, what profit is it if we slay our brother and conceal his blood? *Come, and let us sell him to the Ishmaelites, and let not our hand be upon him; for he is our brother and flesh. And his brethren were content. Then there passed by Midianites merchantmen, and they drew and lifted Joseph out of the pit, and sold Joseph to the Ishmaelites for twenty pieces of silver: and they brought Joseph into Egypt."*

Genesis 37:26-28

The first time Reuben spoke to them, they had Joseph thrown into an empty well. He would certainly die if he had been in the well for long, and God's plans for him would still be cut short. However, the Lord needed to speak through Judah this time; he saw some Ishmaelite passing by and felt they should sell him to them instead of killing him. So, again, God spared the life of Joseph. Now, there's a twist here that I would love us to note. When Reuben spoke the first time to stop them from killing him, he had an ulterior motive; he wanted to go back later to pull him out of the well to deliver him to his father. But he was disappointed to discover that his brothers had double-crossed him to sell out earlier before he got there.

The truth is that Reuben would stand in the way of God. Undoubtedly good motive, but he was wrong; you know why? God's plan was for Joseph to be sold to Egypt, suffer in Egypt, and become dogged in the jungle of destiny pursuit so that he can be fit for the task ahead. God's plan was for Joseph to be stripped of his coat of many colors (comfort) and his comfort zone. God wanted him to go through the wilderness, deserts, waters, fires, and lack to show him how he would handle terrible situations like that. So, Reuben did not understand where God was going with Joseph.

However, Judah's intervention was needed to transport Joseph to his next school of destiny. Therefore, God will eventually preserve your future every step of the way.

The Enemy's Assumption of your Destiny

Have you heard people discuss someone like nothing good seems to be happening for the person, and they are happy to see them in that condition? On the other hand, some people's lives sometimes go into what I call **"temporary obscurity,"** and the people around them wonder if they still exist. Some lose their jobs, others have fire burn down their shops, and some get dumped by their spouse and are almost going into depression and other challenges. In conditions like this, it's easy for the enemy to assume he's defeated you. But let's examine what the brothers of Joseph told their father.

"And he knew it and said, it is my son's coat; **an evil beast hath devoured him;** *Joseph is, without doubt, rent in pieces."*

Genesis 37:33

They assumed that an animal had devoured him, meaning it had killed him. Isn't that their actual plan from the beginning? The truth is that they felt Joseph was going to die in slavery. Therefore, they assume that there is no way he can come out of slavery and possibly have his dreams fulfilled.

The devil's desire over our lives is to see us completely submerged in the ocean of pain and frustration, but God is always ahead of us.

God was Involved

"And the Midianites sold him into Egypt unto Potiphar, an officer of Pharaoh's and captain of the guard."

Genesis 37:36

Somehow Joseph landed in Potiphar's house in Egypt. From the home when Jacob sent him to check on his brother on the field, when Joseph was stripped of his coat of many colors, to when he was thrown into the pit, to when he was brought out of the hole and sold out to the Ishmaelite, and now to Potiphar in Egypt.

You notice that God was with Joseph at each point in this journey and fully involved in every occurrence. All we need in life is to ensure God is delighted in us and our actions. He knows all that we go through. God understands how terrible the journey has been. He's still watching. He's not blind to what others want to do to you; He sees them all. Will you trust Him?

Chapter 3

JOSEPH PROSPERED IN SLAVERY

Genesis 39: 1 – 6

God desires nothing less for you than to grow to your full potential.
**Sébastien Richard, 5 Reasons God Wants
You to Prosper**

Slavery is one condition of life we all hate with a passion. For those subjected to some form of slavery in the past, you can relate to this effectively. For those who have had to stay with an uncle or work as a maid in a wicked rich man's house, where you had no say, and you were despitefully used and possibly subjected to molestation by wife and children, you should connect with what Joseph went through as an enslaved person. The truth is that there is no dignity in enslaved persons. Every enslaved person is limited in what they can do in their Master's house.

In the early days, men and women like Beecher Stowe, Frederick Douglass, Sojourner Truth, Tubman Harriet, John Brown, Olaudah Equiano, and many others stood up against slavery. These guys went through slavery as some of them were enslaved. They saw it all; they went through hell and couldn't sit back to watch the injustice continue; hence, they rose to the challenge. Some lost their lives in the process, and some went to jail. No one will ever go through slavery, and I pray for even their enemy to endure it. Now you can imagine what Joseph was subjected to; evil isn't it?

For Joseph, it was a unique experience entirely. One reoccurring statement about Joseph's experience in slavery was that God was with him. In other words, God watched him become enslaved and saw no reason to stop him from going through the experience. Do you know why? God had an agenda; there was a divine plan in what looked like regression to a normal human eye.

In this section, we shall look at how Joseph prospered in slavery and how he became a leader and a manager even in slavery.

God's presence makes the Difference.

"And the Lord was with Joseph, and he was a prosperous man, and he was in the house of his master the Egyptian."

Genesis 39:2

The dictionary defines prosperity as the condition of success and good fortune. But can you say Joseph had good luck in this instance? Would you, on the middle ground, call slavery prosperity? Think about this for a while! The Difference here was the Presence of God. The Presence of God is all a man needs in his life to break limits. But what exactly is the Presence of God?

Christians frequently quote Exodus 33:14, stating, "And He said, my presence will go with thee, and I will grant you rest." One subject that comes up frequently in church services and Christian gatherings is the "Presence of God,"; but unlike Joseph, many of us may be lacking the Presence of God in our lives. However, a Christian's daily life has been described as being protected by the invisible Presence of God. Although some religious sects argue this, this argument is not incorrect because it is confirmed in the Scriptures that God's Presence ultimately guards and protects anyone sheltered under it. The advantages of spending time in God's Presence as outlined in Psalm 91; let's look at the verses below.

Ps.91:1

"He that dwells in the secret place of the highest shall abide under the shadow of the Almighty."

Ps.91:11–12

"For He shall give His angels charge over you, to keep thee in all thy ways. They shall bear thee up in their hands, lest thou dash thy foot against a stone."

What precisely might be referred to as God's Presence?

God is omnipresent, meaning He is everywhere, and the world is filled with His Presence. He observes everything we do, and nothing escapes His notice. Yes! God is everywhere, yet his presence is more significant than anything else; Joseph had an excellent experience of this overwhelming reality.

Joseph was conscious of God and His might in the Presence of God. When there is a relationship between a person and God, the

Presence of God is inevitably released on such a person. A person with a relationship with God is entirely aware of the dynamics of the Holy Spirit and the actions He takes with others. You recall we talked about Joseph having a personal relationship with God earlier. This relationship is what guarantees God's Presence. God is with us at all times. God gives us His spirit, which is with us and in us when we put our faith in Jesus (see John 14:16-17). However, it can be challenging to acknowledge his presence when we are not connected with the Spirit of God.

So, in our dispensation, the Holy Spirit is the abiding Presence of God in us. We must crave to partner with Him if we make it through life's challenges as Joseph did. For young people to go through their life journey in this sinful world, they'll need the Holy Spirit. The anchor verse says; "And God was with Joseph…." The question is, where is God in slavery? How would I say God is with me when I'm suffering? How would you say God is with you when you hardly afford a meal in a day? Aren't these the questions we ask ourselves most time?

One thing you can afford to miss in life is the Presence of God. See, you may lose money, business, family, friendship, or even reputation, but don't lose the Presence of God. Joseph lost virtually everything dear to him; family, his coat of many colors, his pride, his freedom, his Father's love, and many others, but he made sure he had God with him. The defining factor in a man's life is the Presence of God in their life. So how do I enjoy the Presence of God in my life's journey?

Come Clean with God and Accept Jesus Fully in your Life. Sometimes a communication barrier prevents you from God's presence. Joseph never lacked that dimension of romance with

God's Presence. But some of us feel this way most time. It's a fact that He is still present, but don't you think that un-confessed sin in your life may impact your sensitivity to His Presence?

When I remain silent (about his sin), my bones are worn out from my moaning all day long, the psalmist David remarked. So, if you have any evil or flaw in your heart, confess it to feel God's presence fully. It will help you to activate your awareness of His Presence fully.

Of course, entering via the door of the spiritual life (Jesus Christ) is crucial in developing this close relationship with God. We re-establish contact with the Spirit of our Creator Heavenly Father and grow more conscious of His presence when our human nature is born again. You can continuously sense God's Presence in all circumstances, including moments of joy and sadness, contentment and difficulty in the following ways:

1. Deal with the Sinful Nature as a Born-Again Child of God

Sometimes you find out that even after accepting Jesus as our Lord and personal Savior, we keep battling with certain things. These things keep coming between God and us.

Sin poisons our communion with God. Rom.6.23 says, "For the wages of sin is death, but the gift of God is eternal life through Jesus Christ our Lord." God knows sin shatters our relationship with Him. Hence, He commands us not to sin. Sin has a way of weakening us spiritually. Apostle Paul lamented in Romans when he said he keeps doing things he hates. As young guys, one fundamental thing that contends with our relationship with God is easily besetting sins. Those so-called little foxes are capable of eating up the vine.

If we hide sin in our hearts, God won't listen to our prayers (Psalm 66:18). We must do everything possible to abstain from all appearances of evil. Obtain grace from God to stay pure so you can enjoy God's Presence. We shall talk more about purity later on in this book.

2. Take Studying the Scriptures Very Seriously

God's word quickens and energizes. David said he keeps God's word in his heart so that he won't sin against God (Ps 119:11). Jesus said the words He speaks to us are Spirit and Life (John 6:63). Develop the habit of reciting and declaring God's word in affirmation. You'll undoubtedly feel God's Presence when you give time to studying His word consistently. Questions are, how often do we look at God's word? Why should we study God's word? When did you learn God's word last? Do you only read it when you go to church? If you take God's word seriously, God will take you seriously.

3. Spend time meditating Daily.

Meditation is critical to enjoying God's Presence. We are advised to meditate on God's word day and night so that our souls can prosper (Joshua 1:8). Our inner man thrives when we spend time with God, reflecting on vital issues and fellowshipping with him. Meditation is essential to reaching God; it unlocks your soul and opens you to divine connectivity. Deep meditation takes you to realms beyond human intellect and launches you into the realm of power and divine wisdom. That was the type of wisdom Joseph displayed that Pharaoh had no option but to make him the prime minister; that was indeed the wisdom of the Holy Ghost.

Have you spent time meditating today?

4. Consistent Prayers

One way to have a remarkable communion with God is through prayer. It's two-way communication. You talk to God, and he speaks to you. Prayer is simply a kind of fellowship with God. You have not prayed if you pray and do not feel God's presence. When Solomon finished praying while dedicating the temple, the Presence of God came down, and even the priest could not enter the temple to perform his duty. This is because God's glory was so heavy; that's what it means to pray in God's abiding presence.

Have you prayed today?

5. Sing Praise, Worship, Psalms, and Hymns before Him

There's power in praising God. The only spiritual exercise the Bible recorded that is done in heaven is praise and worship. Angels are continually busy worshipping the King of kings and the Lord of Lords. So, whenever we praise God on earth, we replicate what's going on in heaven; this is why you experience heaven when you truly worship God from your heart, and His Presence comes down on you.

The above ways may not be the only ones, but you can explore others to help you grow close to God.

Joseph Prospered

"And the Lord was with Joseph, and he was a prosperous man, and he was in the house of his master the Egyptian."

Genesis 39:2

But remember, Joseph wouldn't prosper but in God's presence. Indeed, he had nothing at the time, but he had God. He was an embodiment of God's glory. He was a carrier of God's presence. Little wonder, nothing could stop him! God's presence undoubtedly guarantees prosperity. Do you desire the type of prosperity that knows no boundary?

Have you heard someone say, I'm a great man, and those around him looked at themselves and, of you, a great man? They probably can't see any trace of greatness in them. How would you look at someone who has nothing and can hardly handle their basic needs and call him prosperous? How would you reconcile the fact that they are currently living in penury with being a great man? Joseph, the Bible clearly states that he was a prosperous man in the house of his Master. Isn't that a contrast? It was more like saying he was a successful but enslaved man. In other words, he was a **prosperous enslaved person**. To the eye of an ordinary human being, it doesn't add up at all! Seek the presence of God. Joseph carried God's presence that was not hidden from those around him.

We are a world that defines prosperity by influence and affluence, a society that has relegated prosperity to material wealth, the number of certificates acquired, cars, houses, and other mundane things of this world. Look at that scripture again; "….and he was a prosperous man…." The truth is, how do you mean Joseph was a prosperous man? Does it look like it?

The subject of prosperity, like success, has been marginally discussed. Worth is sometimes discussed in isolation with other essential parameters for measuring success.

If it doesn't contain affluence and wealth, it's not success. God's yardstick for measuring success is undoubtedly different from our human parameters. Now let's view this thing this way. Why do you think Joseph was tagged "A Prosperous Man" in slavery? The reason is not farfetched; God's perspective of success and prosperity differs from ours. To God, you've succeeded when you do well in any assignment he gives you. He sees you as prosperous when you keep growing in anything he's asked you to do.

Try as much as possible not to want to be like everybody. Some of us try to be like others and end up being nothing. Let's get this right; if you stay long on course enough, focusing on what God wants you to do, you'll undoubtedly succeed. Don't ever feel inferior to anybody. No! Later in this book, you'll discover Joseph stayed on course; God was involved in the journey.

You see, some of our young ones are easily thrown off-balance when they hear that a friend is traveling abroad to study either medicine, law, pharmacy, accounting, and so on; they start to look down on themselves probably because they are learning a supposed "lower course" compared to that of their friends. Sometimes, they never know that the same course they are studying will be the connecting factor to somewhere far above what any of their other friends are looking for. What you learn sometimes isn't the end but a means to an end. Specific experiences are a by-product of our lives; life's journey makes us go through them, but they don't define who we are. You must know this! Never allow anything or anyone to make you feel less of yourself, be confident of whom God has e you to be.

The Master's Testimony

"And his master saw that the Lord was with him and made all he did to prosper in his hand." Genesis 39:3

This section is so powerful that you must pay keen attention to every word. You'll undoubtedly get profound insight as you read. So let us get right into it as I ask you a few questions; what made you leave the last place of employment; were you sacked or resigned? What legacy did you leave behind when you were leaving? For those of us who are students, what do your classmates say about you? What exactly do they call you in class? What do they see in you? For those of us who are in business, what do your business colleagues call you? Do they see you as a different entity in terms of your heavenly identity? Do you have a good report among them? Is the name of God glorified by your actions? Too many questions, right?

Now let's analyze the scriptures above.

"And the master saw…." What is your boss at work seeing in you? What can your boss say about you? Potiphar testified of Joseph; he saw God in Joseph. Some of us work in an environment where people can tell if you're of God. Some of us live in such a way that people can hardly identify us with Christ. The critical thing in the case of Joseph was that an unbeliever saw Christ in him, an unbelieving boss, in short. Isn't that an excellent testimony of an "ordinary" enslaved person?

Now, if your superior appraise you, what will he say about you? Potiphar did not hand over his entire house to Joseph for no reason; he saw something and God in him. Godliness is essential for our generation; we need to maintain a lifestyle of Jesus that is void of ambiguity and double standards.

The Bible calls us the salt and light of the earth (Matthew 5:13). We are advised to let our shine bright so men around us can see our good works and glorify the Father in us (Matthew 5:16). Paul also quoted Prophet Isaiah, and advised that we shouldn't let the name of God be blasphemed through us among the gentiles (Isaiah 52:5, Romans 2:24). People should see us and see God just like Joseph did. Are you aspiring to live a life that will be very fulfilling and glorious like that of Joseph? Let the world see Jesus in you; don't hide your identity wherever you go. Choose to live for Jesus and Jesus alone. However, it is also good to note that not all may praise you for what God is doing through you. They may be jealous of what God is doing in your life. Leave them alone, strife to be the best version of yourself in the Presence of God and magnify Him always. The Master of masters, our heavenly Father, is counting on you. What can God say about you? God testified of Job even to the devil. What can God say about you? My prayer is that when all is done on this, you will be able to receive these words from our Lord Jesus Christ, *"Well done, good and faithful servant."* Matthew 25:21.

Favor with Man and Favour with God

And Joseph found grace in his sight and served him: He made him overseer over his house and that entire he had put into his hand. And it came to pass from the time that he had made him overseer in his house, and over all that he had, that the Lord blessed the Egyptian's house for Joseph's sake; and the blessing of the Lord was upon all that he had in the place, and the field. And he left all that he had in Joseph's hand; and he knew not ought he had, save the bread which he did eat. And Joseph was a goodly person and well-favored. Genesis 39:4-6

His Master had no choice at this moment but to align with what he was seeing in the life of Joseph. See, man will be compelled to favor you when God is in action in your life. Take a look at what the verse says again; "And Joseph found grace (favor in his (master's) sight……." A man who has already found favor with God will always find favor with ith men. God's blessing produces men's turn, and men's vogue brings physical realities of our daily living. How do I know that? The Bible says his Master handed over the operation of the entire house to him. Sometimes I wonder how a man like Potiphar, the Chief of Defense Staff to Pharaoh, handed over all his businesses to an enslaved person like Joseph, a young boy from a foreign land.

Earlier on, we talked about how God was with Joseph and how he enjoyed the Presence of God; that was God's favor. God so much favored him that even those around him could see it; His Master could see that God was with him; what a privilege!

Joseph became a manager instead of an enslaved person. What a favor! God can do this in anyone who cares to live by His will. Joseph prospered in God's favor. I pray that the blessing of God will locate in all aspects of your life in the name of Jesus. Amen!

Chapter 4

JOSEPH PASSED THE TESTS FOR GREATNESS

Genesis 39: 5 – 13; 41:16

Great testimonies are the outcome of great tests.
Great triumphs can only come out of great trials.
Smith Wigglesworth

The story of Joseph, especially in light of his rise to power, intrigues everyone. Of course, we all love to associate with such stories. Stories like this fuel, rekindle, ignite our minds, and whet our appetites for more extraordinary things. No doubt God was with Joseph. God was involved for an enslaved person to become more like a family member and a group managing director of Pharaoh Holdings. At this point, Joseph has begun to flourish again, enjoying many benefits and privileges. He was in charge of all businesses, prepared payroll for other servants, determined who got a salary increase, and kept records of all transactions. The master knew nothing about how much he was worth but Joseph. Can you imagine that? Having such people around you is good, especially if you are a leader. Currently, I serve in Tenwek Hospital College – School of chaplaincy. I have an Administrative Assistant. There is one thing among others that I admire in Caroline Sambai. When it comes to finances and accounting for whatever she is given, there is no question about it. I have always felt at peace when I assign her anything financial that requires proper accountability. She does it the best. As a leader, I am proud of her, and I pray that we will have such people around us and that we will all be the same in the presence of God so that he can entrust us with great things on this earth.

Some believers may have accepted Potiphar's house as their final rest, just like Joseph was becoming too comfortable in slavery. This is a junction we must all be cautious lest we settle for less and decide to maintain the status quo. Joseph was entirely in charge, but that wasn't the final bus stop; yes, he prospered in slavery, but total freedom awaited him. I imagine him comparing where his dreams were at this time. Imagine him saying to himself; is this really what I saw? No matter how great I am here, I'm still a slave. The question is, how will he navigate his way from here to his destiny? How will he emerge into that giant he saw? How will he become a custodian of God's grace? In my second year at Kenya Highlands Bible College, we had a great preacher named Dr. Gilbert Egerton. He came to preach to us during the Revival emphasis week. I remember the theme of his message, "Don't settle for less than God's best – Believe for more." That statement has remained with me for years, and I believe I should stick to it daily. I think Joseph needed such encouragement at that time.

This chapter will delve deep into the prerequisites for being a custodian of God's grace, which I call; "Tests for success." Every believer who wants to climb the ladder of elegance to the top must pass these three tests. Your emergence solely depends on what you do when facing these tests. The situation around Joseph was such that he could easily fall or fail these three tests, but he passed them all.

God is still looking for young people to trust with grace. Can God trust you? Let's get right into it as we look at how Joseph escaped falling for these temptations and trials.

1. The test of Integrity

Integrity is a spiritual course. Unfortunately, believers need to realize this more so they can study the trail hard to avoid failing the course; the danger is that you must pass the course to advance into the next phase in your spiritual journey. Our God is a God of principles and systems; He has systematically calved out a path for us to tread so we can ascend the throne of power and glory. Joseph understood this very well; hence, he patiently endured the pain and demeaning situations to become what God had destined him to be.

Our world today is full of falsehoods, false lives, false certificates, false marriages, and much cheating and lying here and there. Sometimes you ask, where is our conscience? Do we still fear God? Have you not discovered that most people who forge certificates to get a job, cheat in an examination, reduce their age to get a job, steal money in offices, and lie to superiors are Christians? If you think I lie, do your research. One of the reasons we lack genuine experience of the supernatural is primarily due to reasons like this. God is finding it difficult to trust us; heaven is careful, so we won't deceive people with even anointing.

What is Integrity?

The dictionary defines Integrity as steadfast adherence to a strict moral or ethical code. You know this is correct and stick to it no matter what. Risk maintaining specific biblical standards even when everyone in the office is against you. You instead purpose for any eventuality like Mordecai than compromise divine principles. Until you get to this point with God, you are not fit to become a Prime Minister in a foreign land or success in the path of your destiny.

Now let's look at how Joseph maintained his Integrity in Potiphar's house.

"And it came to pass from the time that he had made him overseer in his house, and over all that he had, that the Lord blessed the Egyptian's house for Joseph's sake; and the blessing of the Lord was upon all that he had in the house, and the field. And he left all that he had in Joseph's hand; and knew not ought he had, save the bread which he did eat. And Joseph was a goodly person and well favored."

Genesis 39:5-6

Now let's extract a few facts so we can adequately explore what God is trying to teach us through the life of Joseph in these verses.

- » Joseph made an **"Overseer."**
- » **Overall**, he had.
- » God blessed the master's business for Joseph's sake.
- » There was **an increase (Profit)** at home and on the field.

- » He **left it all** in Joseph's hand.
- » **His master didn't even have a record of what he had at some point.** Potiphar only knows when they give him food.
- » Joseph was a good person.

Can you see what I'm seeing? This is so marvelous that I feel excited when I keenly look at the highlighted part of the points. Joseph became the overseer; wow! He became the Managing Director of Potiphar's Holdings in Egypt; He controlled all that his master had and ensured an increase in profit as he served his master. As a result, the master decided to hand over not just the business but everything, including the house. He was in charge of farm animals, crops, housekeeping, and other servants and maids on the field and domestic staff. Can you see how mighty he had become?

Now begin to imagine Joseph in our contemporary time. He would be a group managing director; in charge of several companies; what an extensive portfolio! But I need to find a way to go. My focus is on how well he represented God in Potiphar's house. Joseph kept the house, and there was no record of embezzlement. Even though his master knew not what he had, Joseph did not begin to hide some crops or animals to enrich himself secretly. No! He did no such thing. Of course, he could steal, and his master wouldn't even notice it, but he never did.

Retake a look at those verses. The scripture says the master left all in his hand. His master wouldn't even audit him since he had no record of transactions. Joseph knew this, but he chose to lead a life of Integrity than amass wealth that will leave you, or you will leave it. Joseph effectively passed his test; have you passed yours? Yes, this man of God did not want to fail his God; he had seen where

God was taking him long before, but he needed to pass this integrity test to be fully qualified for the throne.

How did you handle your lifting the last time you were promoted? Have you suddenly joined the league of the big boys in the company, a guy who adds zeros to zeros to defraud the organization? Have you begun to sign unnecessary allowances for useless trips for yourself so you can siphon money? Yes, you pray and even officiate in the church; you cry to God to make you the Joseph of your generation; beloved, can you possibly become a Joseph of our time with soiled hands?

Galatians 6:7 says, "Do not be deceived; God is not mocked; for whatever a man sows, he will also reap." You lie on your bed the way you lay it. You can't plant beans and reap maize. That is practically not possible. So, to become a Joseph in our generation, you must pass the integrity test and other required tests.

2. The test of Purity

Generally, the scriptures admonish us to keep ourselves pure like God. If we hope to make it to heaven when the master returns to take the saints home (1 John 3:3). Our God is pure. Prophet Habakkuk tells us that the eyes of God are too pure to see iniquity (Habakkuk 1:13); that was why he had to turn away from Jesus when he was dying on the cross for the sins of the whole world. If God couldn't bear to see His own Son carry our sins on the cross, why would you think He would condone our sins? Purity is one criterion heaven can't compromise when searching for generational deliverers. This is a standard that God himself has set, for He is not a man the can lie. He always keeps his word. Joseph again passed the purity test, but how did he do it? Let's read these verses.

"And it came to pass after these things that his master's wife cast her eyes upon Joseph, and she said, lie with me. But he refused and said unto his master's wife, behold, my master would not know what is with me in the house, and he hath committed all that he hath to my hand; there is none more significant in this house than I; neither hath he kept back anything from me but thee, because thou art his wife: how then can I do this great wickedness and sin against God? And it came to pass, as she spoke to Joseph day by day, that he hearkened not unto her, to lie by her, or to be with her. And it came to pass that Joseph went into the house to do his business, and there was none of the men of the house there within. And she caught him by his garment, saying, lie with me: He left his garment in her hand, fled, and got him out. And it came to pass when she saw that he had left his garment in her hand and was run forth."

Genesis 39:7-13

A time came when Potiphar's wife cast her eyes on Joseph with lustful desire. She made her demand clear to Joseph; "lie with me," she said to him, but Joseph declined her request. When we read this story on the surface, we may appreciate the lessons here more than we should. You will need to look at the tale from the contemporary point of view.

Now, let's look at it this way. Joseph was a personal aid to the Chief of Defense Staff to a nation's national governor al government. His boss acknowledges the grace upon his life we saw earlier; the master had also handed over everything he had in his hand except his wife. What do you think would be going through the mind of Joseph when his master's wife said to him, "lie with me?" He would need clarification on what to do. Who will he report such a thing to, being a slave? Who would believe Joseph against his master's wife? What exactly can he do to stop his master's wife? Now pause reading this book and think about this for a while!

Some guys would jump at the opportunity. After all, they could be making more money while servicing the woman. This is one reason some young guys and girls end up with sugar mummies and daddies. Some are trapped in some foreign countries living with significantly older women to make money. Joseph understood divine principles; if I let myself hooked down by this woman, my dreams would be forever shattered. So I imagine Joseph telling him; I want to take advantage of the heavenly agenda.

See, there's something more I want to share here. Do you know that saying "NO" to Potiphar's wife would probably not be the first time Joseph would say no to sexual sin? Don't forget there were hundreds of maids working with him on the field and in the house; you also recall that he controls and manages them all. Do you think some of these girls may not have tried to seduce him in one way or another? Joseph had the power to tell any of them; to meet me in my room tonight, and they wouldn't object to it, but he did not do such a thing. So, Joseph had made the decision not to accept long before Potiphar's wife made her attempt. Certain sins come in bunches. It begins small, and if you fight it from the word go, the strength to withstand the upcoming evils will be more durable, and thus the momentum is created even for future challenges.

Many young boys and girls still battle sexual sins; some will cry, and even they promise they won't repeat it but find themselves soon after. Some who sing in a choir don't see anything wrong with premarital sex, yet we want to sing, and miracles will happen; how's that possible? Joseph passed the test of sexual sins; have you passed yours?

Beloved, it would be best if you did everything possible to overcome this temptation. The scripture says that every sin a man commits is without the body, but the sin of fornication is against your soul. Joseph knew this. Hence, he said, "I can't do this wickedness against my master and God." You must get to the level in your walk with God where you allow the word of God in your heart to help you defeat the internal cravings of the flesh. You don't just let your flesh get whatever it wants. Paul said, **"I beat my body, and I bring it under subjection;** lest after I might have preached to others, I become a castaway." The critical thing here is that he beats his body and puts it under control. It is your job to engage the fruit of self-control. You have to call God for grace. Be determined not to let the devil soil your testimony. Joseph passed the test; are you determined to pass yours?

3. The test of pride

Joseph was a humble man when he was dealing with Potiphar and Pharaoh.

"And Joseph answered Pharaoh, saying, it is not in me: God shall give Pharaoh an answer of peace."

Genesis 41:16

Now come to think of it, a favored man, who has transformed from being an enslaved person into a manager, a man has been put in charge of all that his master has, and a man who now has absolute power to command and declare anything in his master's house. It is easy for such a man to naturally become proud, especially when his master attested openly that God was with him and praised him in front of others; Joseph could have been proud if he wanted to. Still, he refused to let the praises of men get to him.

Joseph did not begin to boss people around because he was in charge. One thing that touched me was his reply to Pharaoh in

Genesis 41:16. He told the king that he wasn't the one to interpret dreams but God. Joseph recognized that God gave him the ability to analyze the dream, and Joseph knew how to point people to God and not himself.

How often do you take glory for what God does through you? How often do you become so high-minded because you are elevated at work? Can God trust you with so much grace for more incredible things? Don't you know God resists the proud and gives grace to the humble? Joseph was humble; how humble are you?

Chapter 5

JOSEPH PAID THE PRICE OF GREATNESS

Genesis 39: 17 – 23

You can only become great at that thing you're willing to sacrifice for.
Maya Angelou

Greatness is something almost everyone wants to get hold of and enjoy forever. I love the wind of greatness and admire it with all my breath. But wait a minute, is this worth going for? I never knew how expensive greatness would be. As I continue to learn from those who have walked this path, I have realized that it is a costly encounter. But, of course, there is genuine greatness as well as fake greatness. It is good to note that real greatness lasts while fake one does not.

A young lady was asked why she gave in to a guy who was not born again; her answer was rather touching. She said, "I never intended this for my life, but fellow Christian friends pushed me into this. They kept telling me, 'he's a good guy, gentle, and so on, but you see, I was a fool to have heeded their advice. Look at it today, I'm pregnant, and my husband has traveled abroad with another woman; what can I do now? I must live with this the rest of my life."

While she said all this, tears rolled down the eyes of those there. Earlier in life, God had already shown her the type of man she would marry; she had rejected a lot of playboys, including the one she later fell for. The guy joined the church to get her, and he succeeded. She saw the signals but could not maintain her position by reasons of the pressure from her friends. She wanted to belong because it looked like her friends were pulling away from her. But she couldn't pay the price to stand out!

To become the odd man/woman for God in our generation, you have to sacrifice dearly to become that. This section will again examine Joseph's life in terms of the sacrifice he had to pay to maintain purity, integrity, and loyalty. We hope this will spur us into action after learning from this hero.

Accused and Prosecuted for no Reason

Have you been indicted for something you know nothing about? Have you been called a thief and know you stole nothing from anybody? Has anyone lied against you, and the whole world thinks it's true? Have you attempted to defend yourself, and it's not looking like you'll get out of it soon? Are you so disturbed by the outright injustice meted against you because of your faith in Christ?

Or are you almost giving up because you can no longer bear it? Sometimes, we may think all will be well because we are doing the right things. It is sometimes different.

Well, I've got good news for you; all things are working together for your good because you're walking within the will of the Father. Joseph was never ultimately disappointed; similarly, God will not disappoint you if you walk in his path. The passage we looked at earlier stated that Potiphar's wife mounted pressure on Joseph daily; of course, Joseph couldn't have opened up to anybody since he was a mere enslaved person. Joseph was, however, determined not to give in to his master's wife. So, a time came when the woman advanced beyond mere word and made a physical attempt on him; while Joseph tried to talk her out of it, she was rather adamant. Joseph then explores the last option he has left; he runs out of the room, leaving his jacket in her hand. Joseph would've told her, "I can't come this far only to end up like this. I can't let the pleasure of five minutes rob me of the big picture. I can let go of my jacket, but not my destiny."

Potiphar's wives are everywhere; how often do you run from them? They are at school, in your class, at the marketplaces, in various offices, and virtually in every circle of influence. Would it be foolish to let them strip you of your enviable future? Joseph stood his ground for God, but was that all? Not at all! He had to pay a considerable price to stand for God. His master's wife decided to claim an attempted rape against Joseph instead of her advances toward Joseph. You can solve the puzzle of what would become of Joseph in a situation like this; how will he defend himself against his master's wife? What will an ordinary enslaved person convince people against the madam of the house?

Joseph has been indicted at this point, and there was nothing he could do to salvage the situation. He was immediately sent prosecuted without a fair hearing. An enslaved person truly has no say in the house of his master! Do you know Potiphar could doubt whether his wife is telling the truth? But it will be a slap on the wife's face if he dares to make his distrust obvious. So, Joseph was indicted and prosecuted for no reason. Again, the question is, where was God when this was happening? He was undoubtedly on his throne, watching the wickedness of men.

Jailed for No Reason

"And she spoke unto him according to these words, saying, The Hebrew servant, whom thou hast brought unto us, came in unto me to mock me:

And it came to pass, as I lifted my voice and cried, that he left his garment with me and fled out. And it came to pass when his master heard the words of his wife, which she spoke unto him, saying after this manner did thy servant to me; **that his wrath was kindled. And Joseph's master took him and put him into the Prison, where the king's prisoners were bound: and he was there in Prison."**

Genesis 39:17-21

Potiphar got furious and ordered that Joseph be bounded and thrown into Prison. There was no chance for enslaved people to defend themselves before being prosecuted. He was immediately judged in the negative direction. Joseph should've said, "God, this was not what I saw; is this how I will end up? I refused to compromise because I fear you; should I die because of that? Can you help me, Lord? Why should I die for doing the right thing?

Now let's look at it this way. Have you been indicted for something you know nothing about? Some of you will recall those times in school when that guy lied against you; and how you felt incapacitated for not being able to get justice. Seriously, it could be very frustrating. If care is not taken, it can make you do what you shouldn't do. Some have gone into a depression because of such situations, especially when they can see or sense where it will land them. Some had even committed suicide instead of going through the shame and the pain of being a prisoner.

It was apparent that Joseph would die, but God again set in at the right time to make sure his sentencing was reduced to imprisonment, and Joseph was eventually jailed for no reason. See, I don't know what is done against you to imprison your life and destiny, but God will vindicate you. The Satanic set-ups are here; the devil keeps scheming against God's children at every opportunity. This is why believers must always be on guard to avoid an error. In the case of Joseph, it was entirely out of his hands to save himself, but God did not disappoint him.

Standing for Jesus at any time will always cost you something. So always be ready for the aftermath whenever you must stand for God. The three Hebrew Guys saw the fire but were prepared to suffer and die. God is always interested in those who would put their lives on the line for God. Are you one of such?

The Presence of God Cannot be Imprisoned.

You may imprison a man who carries God's presence, but God's existence cannot be imprisoned. Likewise, you may limit someone with God's presence, but you can't restrict the presence of God on them. The presence of God in a person will always manifest anywhere, anytime; the environment is not a barrier to his operations, and his presence can't be tamed.

Take a look at the verse below;

"But the Lord was with Joseph, *and showed him mercy, and gave him favor in the sight of the prison keeper."*

Genesis 39:21

The very first statement here captured it all. It started with "But." The 'but' there shows a deviation from what was going on; the reality was that he was in Prison, everything looked closed, nothing seemed to be working, and death looked imminent. But you know what? The Lord was with Joseph! Being in Prison doesn't naturally show that God was with him. Having no money to go to school may make you feel like God isn't with you, lack of food could make you feel like God isn't with you, and so many other scenarios. For Joseph, the bible says, "but God was with him." What else will a man need if he already has God with him? With God by your side, everything is possible. Now I can see and understand, but there was a time that I could neither see this truth nor understand what was happening around me. When I was about ten years old, and my parent could not take me to school or even provide me with basic needs, everything was dark. I lost hope completely. I could only see a pastor allowing me to stay at his house with his children. I could see a teacher allowing me to stay at his home when he went on holiday. I could see a Principal getting my name to the students who needed financial support.

Little did I know that God was working on the background to make my destiny successful. When I now look back and see the hand of God in all that, I can testify of the Lord's goodness in my personal life. For this reason, I wrote my first book "Stand Out and Be Counted."

The second part of the above scripture says, "……and showed him mercy, and gave him favor in the sight of the prison keeper". God's presence guaranteed Joseph mercy and favor. God showed him mercy and gave him favor with men. The housekeeper also favored him by divine arrangement. In Prison, the compassion and favor of God never left Joseph. I guess someone is encouraged to feel alive again. God's with you, brother; His presence will bring you favor in Jesus' name.

Joseph Prospered again in Prison.

"And the keeper of the Prison committed to Joseph's hand all the prisoners in Prison; and whatsoever they did there, he was the doer of it. **The keeper of the Prison looked not to anything under his hand; because the Lord was with him, and that which he did, the Lord made it to prosper."**

Genesis 39:22-23

As I look at these two verses, I get excited. The presence of God always makes a difference for Joseph. Here again, the warder handed over everything in the Prison to Joseph. Recall that he became Potiphar's holdings' GMD (Group Managing Director). Here again, he has become the foreman to the Prison keeper. Whatever they do in the prison house is done on Joseph's order. What a grace!

God doesn't abandon His children when in trouble; He stays with them and faces their challenges. That's the God we serve. He prospered Joseph again in Prison. But, one may ask, is there prosperity in the Prison? Truth is what looks like a prison to you on the surface is a process for God to prune you and put you in shape for His use.

Yes, Joseph was in Prison, but he prospered in Prison. However, he knew he had far more than a prison leader to offer to his world. Joseph kept pushing with God, ensuring he kept his relationship with God intact because he knew it was the only specific currency to access anything on earth. The Prison was not a barrier in any way. His life in Prison was indeed a fulfilling one.

Chapter 6

JOSEPH'S PRISON EXPERIENCE

Genesis 40: 1 – 23

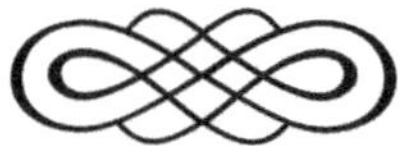

You can jail a Revolutionary, but you can't jail the Revolution.
Huey Newton

Eliot shares his experience in prison for four years. Eliot could have been more delightful. But, apart from restricted movement, loneliness is more than enough punishment. He added, "I was away from my siblings, parents, friends (especially John), bicycle, and regular school classes; it is one experience I don't wish even for an enemy."

You may ask, how did Eliot get to prison?

Eliot arrived at an empty class to study in the evening on campus; he never knew someone was beaten to death by some guys and hidden in the corner of the class shortly before he entered. He saw the guy almost lifeless; he was gone before he could call for help. Later on, a forensic report captured his hand on the neck of the diseased, and he was arrested and jailed for what he did not do.

At the time he was telling the story, he was already out of prison, all thanks to God for helping the law enforcement agents to apprehend the true culprit after four years. But you know what? Eliot had met Jesus in prison before coming out; indeed, it was a divine arrangement to arrest him for God. One very touching thing that happened to him was that he had to drink his urine at some point. That wasn't good at all! To be sincere with you, situations like those have made some people commit suicide. How can you send me to prison for no reason? Joseph faced the same scenario. Joseph was also sent to jail for no reason!

Joseph landed in prison and immediately became the boss by the **Presence of God**. One should've expected him to look downcast and sad; instead, he was active and lively. His disposition helped him maintain a personal atmosphere that enhances divine revelation and wisdom. Though he was in prison, he was free in the Spirit. He became an encourager to other prisoners; that's how our lives should be when in trouble. His life began connecting with other lives in prison, relating with others and helping in one form or another. If you truly have the light (The Presence of God), you can't hide wherever you go; it'll naturally shine forth.

Understanding Relationships

Let me start this section by asking you a question; how do you relate to people? How do you react to those around you when you're tensed up, stressed, and possibly offended? Do you begin to transfer aggression from one person to another? Are you the type that a little challenge gets you off-track quickly?

Let's take a look at how Joseph related to other inmates.

"And Joseph came unto them in the morning, **and looked upon them,** *and, behold, they were sad. And he asked Pharaoh's officers that were with him in the ward of his lord's house,* **saying, wherefore look ye so sadly today?"** Genesis 40:6-7

The highlighted phrases are critical to where we're going in this section. First, Joseph **looked upon them**; in other words, he closely observed them. Only a caring person can do that. For you to notice the look in your neighbor's eyes, you must be very observant. Joseph noticed a sad look on their faces and asked, "what's up with you guys? I see you don't seem happy this morning?" Second, Joseph showed genuine concern for the inmates. Don't forget; these were notable inmates; the Buckler and the Baker. They were guys who served the king in the palace until the king got offended by them and threw them in prison.

The big lesson here is the act of caring for one another. It wasn't by accident that Joseph became great in Egypt; it was a collection of several factors. First, you can only have a caring heart if you are a leader. Joseph showed he had a shepherd's heart; "he asked, why are you looking so sad this morning?" Some of us would look away when we see our neighbors going through difficult times; we avoid taking responsibility for being our brother's keeper; we purposely try not to draw anyone's attention to us. Joseph never did that! He initiated a discussion; he looked after them and eventually became a blessing to them.

Life is all about relationships. God showed an example when he said in Genesis, **"Let us** make man in our image......." My emphasis is on "Let Us." Our God is a God who works in conjunction with the angels. The nature of the Trinity is a testament to the fact that God encourages relationships and walking or working with others to achieve a thing. The easiest way to network with people is to offer help or provide free service. It always pays in the long run.

Christians must learn this principle of networking. It is not excellent practice to look away or shun people when they need you; that little girl in your class or the little girl in your department may be a President's or Governor's wife tomorrow. On the other hand, you may need her to secure a colossal contract tomorrow. Learn to build strategic alliances with people wherever you find yourself; it pays to do that. Joseph cared for his inmates, and it paid off. Will you learn from him? However, it is also good to understand this critical perspective. Don't say, "Let me do this act to this one so that I will get this in the future." Just learn to do your acts of love without expecting anything in return. And the God of heaven will see what you do in secret and reward you in His own perfect and genius ways that are better for us at the appropriate time. Isn't wonderful?

Freedom from the Prison

"And they said unto him, we have dreamed a dream, and there is no interpreter. And Joseph said unto them, do not interpretations belong to God? **Tell me them***; I pray you."*

Genesis 40:8

You could see that Joseph was interested in knowing what was going on with them. It was like the prison had no effect on him, and he was spiritually alert; hence, he could help the other inmates. Joseph was physically in prison but spiritually free. He was confined in a place but had access to deep spiritual insights. His caring attitude soon begins to launch him to proffering solutions to his inmate's challenges. He wasn't only in charge physically; he was spiritually in charge.

As a child of God, it is good to become the class rep, but what you do with the opportunity makes the difference. Joseph was more like the class monitor of the prison; he maximized the opportunity to make sure that he impacted the lives of those around him in jail. Spiritual alertness is one leadership trait you must not joke with if you must go far in life. A good leader must be very good at relating and interacting with people.

Now let's imagine Joseph being resentful towards other inmates. Would he have been able to approach them when he felt they were in a problem? With an existing relationship between Joseph and the other guys, he discovered their challenges and eventually manifested the gift of revelation right there in prison. Are you doing where you are in providing spiritual support to those around you? Joseph was in jail but free to express himself in the Spirit.

Spiritual Relevance in Prison

"And the chief butler told his dream to Joseph, and said to him, in my dream, behold, a vine was before me; and in the vine were three branches: and it was as though it budded, and her blossoms shot forth; and the clusters thereof brought forth ripe grapes: and Pharaoh's cup was in my hand: and I took the

grapes, and pressed them into Pharaoh's cup, and I gave the cup into Pharaoh's hand. And Joseph said unto him, this is the interpretation of it: The three branches are three days: yet within three days shall Pharaoh lift thine head, and restore thee unto thy place: and thou shall deliver Pharaoh's cup into his hand, after the former manner when thou was his butler. But think on me when it shall be well with thee, and show kindness, I pray thee, unto me, and make mention of me unto Pharaoh, and bring me out of this house." Genesis 40:9-14.

To make a mark on earth, you must stay relevant and valuable to those around you. Your impact on the world around you determines the magnitude and duration of your relevance. Are you suitable to the world around you? Joseph became physically and spiritually relevant to those around him in prison. He was relevant to the prison keeper as the keeper was relieved of so much work. Courtesy of Joseph's availability to work, the other inmates got someone to talk to in their times and interpret their dreams. He was not discouraged and became useless to himself and those around him; in other words, the prison did not take spirituality from him. He didn't say, God, why would you let go through this and begin to give in to frustration; no! On the contrary, he overcame the challenge with his head raised high in the Spirit.

Joseph became a dream interpreter to people. Have you ever interpreted someone's dream in your entire life? You may wonder what I mean by being an interpreter of someone's dreams. You see, whenever you become the reason for someone to achieve something, help interpret the person's dream. Any time someone pushes through a thing because of your support, you have helped them to analyze their dream. So again, have you ever interpreted a dream for someone?

However, there's a pitfall you must avoid. When you become relevant to those around you, they will always need you to solve their problems. As a result, you could begin to take advantage of them or try to manipulate such relationships in your favor. Let's see more about this in the next section.

The Human Nature in Joseph

"But think on me when it shall be well with thee, and show kindness, I pray thee, unto me, and make mention of me unto Pharaoh, and bring me out of this house: for indeed I was stolen away out of the land of the Hebrews: and here also have I done nothing that they should put me into the dungeon." Genesis 40:14-15

You've got angry with one uncle or a friend who refused to help even when you can see clearly that he's in a position to do so, or you have seen someone complain about that in the past. We tend to try to depend on a man to lift us out of our challenges than relying on God. Joseph had used his God-given gift to help his fellow inmates, and he felt one good turn deserves another, or I scratched your back; you also have to scratch my back. Joseph said I interpreted your dream, but if you return to the palace, help me walk my way out of this place. I imagine the butler nods his head in agreement to help Joseph when he gets out of prison. The question is, what happened when he got reinstated? Did he ever remember Joseph?

God may have placed Joseph there to interpret their dreams but put him in the palace to help Joseph the way Joseph was expecting him to do. Joseph hoped the butler would find an occasion to mention him before the king to let him know that he's been unjustly treated even by Potiphar and his wife. That never happened because God had His agenda. Instead, God was waiting for the right time to take the best shot and make the ovation louder. And that was what happened.

We must learn to trust God instead of relying on others to help us. Man will always be man, and God will always remain God. The last verse of Genesis 40 says, "……yet, the chief butler did not remember Joseph; but he forgot him" Isn't that bad?

Joseph's Interpretations came to fulfillment.

When you speak by the Spirit of God, you become the oracle of God's kingdom, and He confirms your words. Joseph interpreted the butler and the baker's dreams; it happened as he interpreted it. Let's take a look at the scriptures;

"And it came to pass the third day, which was Pharaoh's birthday, that he made a feast unto all his servants: and he lifted the head of the chief butler and the chief baker among his servants. And he restored the chief butler unto his butlership again, and he gave the cup into Pharaoh's hand: But he hanged the chief baker: as Joseph had interpreted to them. Yet did not the chief butler remember Joseph, but forgot him."

Genesis 40:20-23

Joseph's interpretation got fulfilled. It was very accurate and exact. Indeed, he spoke to them by the Spirit of God! Certain things are spiritually discerned; it takes the Spirit to dig out the things of the Spirit. Joseph operated at a very high level of discernment and revelation; hence, he could decipher profound spiritual realities. Prophet Samuel that no word of mouth fell to the ground, meaning every prophecy he gave was accurate. Many have this ability, but we have not fanned it into flame. The ability to see visions, prophecy, and interpret dreams may reside in us, but our spiritual lifestyles have yet to let them flourish. Indeed, the prison experience was challenging, but Joseph enjoyed God's presence throughout his prison stay. It was an excellent experience for him! Not just because it was great but mainly because God used Joseph to be a solution to people and equally trained him to be what he wanted him to be.

Chapter 7

JOSEPH BECAME MORE THAN A DREAMER

Genesis 37: 5 – 9; 40: 9 – 16; 41: 1 – 7

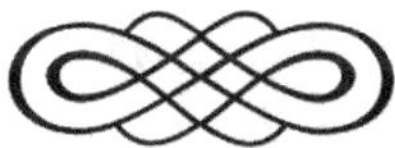

Had Joseph been released when he pleaded for Chief Butler to help him, he would have been working for the Butler and NOT for Pharaoh. Joseph would have been waiting on the Butler instead of Egypt waiting on him. We must learn to trust God, process, and be patient. God's plans are higher and more generous than our own. — **Shaun Brooks**

Every journey in life begins with a dream. And the ability to dream of your future and be clear about it makes your life's journey smooth. So, everyone needs the vision to fulfill their destiny. After achieving it, people often say, "this is a dream come true!" So before getting more profound in this chapter, let's pause to define a dream.

What is a Dream?

According to Wikipedia, a dream is a series of images, concepts, feelings, and experiences that frequently happen uncontrollably in mind during particular sleep phases. Each dream lasts five to twenty minutes, though the dreamer may feel it lasts much longer. Humans dream for roughly two hours each night.

People have sights and sensations in their dreams when they are sleeping. But, according to researchers, each person's dreams include different ideas. They create new scenarios by combining disparate pieces of a person's experiences, concerns, and waking thoughts.

Biblical Definition of a Dream

According to Job 33:15, "In a dream, in a vision of the night, when profound sleep cometh upon mankind, in slumbering upon the bed;" is how a dream is defined in the biblical perspective. This verse from the Bible contains many statements. A dream is, first and foremost, a glimpse from the night. The text also explains that men experience dreams when they sleep deeply. According to the Bible, a vision occurs when a person is awake, whereas a dream occurs when a person is asleep. Some people who research dreams assert that although we constantly dream while sleeping, we only recall our dreams just before waking up. This would line up with the Bible in numerous instances where men remember a dream that jolted them out of sleep.

Recall that in our study of the life of Joseph in this book, we realize that the making of Joseph began with a Dream. The prisoners with him dreamt, and Pharaoh also dreamt. All of these dreams were very significant.

The Dreams

You may be wondering why we have discussed dreams in this book. Dreams are a great instrument in the hand of God, as we saw in the previous sections. God can speak to men through dreams like He communicated His intentions to Joseph about His future, revealed a future occurrence to Pharaoh, and gave the butler and the baker a sense of what would happen through their dreams.

Let's look at each of those dreams as we paraphrase them here.

Joseph's Dreams

Dream 1:

As we were working on the farm and binding sheaves, my sheaf rose and stood straight; yours also rose and stood straight, surrounding my sheaf, but they bowed down to my sheaf. Genesis 37:5

Dream 2:

I have yet another dream; Joseph told his brothers. Again, the sun and moon, alongside eleven stars, bowed to me. Genesis 37:9

Now you'll discover that both dreams are synonymous; the message looks the same. The dreams were so transparent that you didn't need a unique spirit to interpret them. Even his wicked brothers understood it on the surface. But the dreams meant much more than having his parents and siblings bow to him. To God,

Joseph was being prepared to be a generational deliverer, and that was what he saw. Dreams are an essential tool for divine messages.

The Butler's Dream

The chief butler narrated his dream to Joseph and said, I saw a vine appear to me in my dream bringing out three new branches, growing so well and bearing good fruits, and the fruits were ripe. So, I saw myself pressing those grapes into Pharaoh's cup and serving him. Genesis 40:9-11

Now the interpretation Joseph gave was so on point. And it happened precisely how Joseph interpreted it. Joseph told him; three branches were three days, and he would be restored to his position in three days. This interpretation happened precisely the way Joseph said it. Aren't dreams important?

The Baker's Dream

I was also in my dream and saw three white baskets of fruits on my head; inside the caskets had various fruits, but birds came and ate up the fruits on my head. Gen 40:16-17

Of course, this dream sounds terrible. Joseph also interpreted this negatively, which happened just as Joseph interpreted it. The chief baker was brought out of the prison but hung on a tree afterward.

Pharaoh's Dreams

Dream 1:

Pharaoh dreamt and saw himself by the riverside; there, he saw seven fat cows come out of the river and feed around the river; he then saw another seven ugly and gaunt-looking cows come out of the same river and eat up big cows. Genesis 41:1-4

Dream 2:

The same night Pharaoh had another dream; seven heads of grain grew out on a stalk, plump and good. Another seven thin heads sprang up after them, and the seven light heads devoured the seven fat heads.

Genesis 41:5-7

These dreams would be the saving grace of generations, and God found a way to reveal them even to a king with no covenant connection with God. But you know what? The king was limited as to what the dream meant. Yes, he saw it but could not understand what he saw. So, at this junction, are all dreams revelations?

Are All Dreams Revelations?

Going by the definition of dreams above, we can say that all dreams are not revelations. For example, Jerry was a young boy in a boarding school. He was assigned a top bunk to sleep on in the hostel. Jerry plays football often with other students during breaks. He loved football so much that even in his dreams, he kept playing football. One night, as he was playing football in his dream, he threw his leg and physically raised his leg on the top bunk, and fell from the bed. Other students who were yet to sleep and were still reading heard him call Mike, saying, "Mike, pass, pass, give quickly, before falling from the bunk. Would you call that dream a revelation? Not at all! He only dreamt based on a multitude of thoughts and activities. But look at the definition we discussed in Job 33:14-16.

"For God may speak in one way or another, yet man does not perceive it. In a dream, in a vision of the night, when deep sleep falls upon them while slumbering on their beds. Then He opens the ears of men and seals their instruction."

This passage admits that God tries to talk to a man in other ways, but when he sees that man is too busy to listen, He waits until night when they are asleep to instruct them through dreams. God still speaks through dreams. However, all dreams are not revelations. Joseph, the father of Jesus, was told by God through a dream not to divorce Mary because the child in her womb was of the Holy Ghost. Peter was spoken to by God Himself through a dream at Joppa about Cornelius. The list is endless! God is still revealing his mind to His children through dreams. When last did you have a revelation through a dream?

Personal Intimacy with God Defines your Dreams

The magnitude of your intimacy with God defines whether your dream is a mere collection of during-the-day activities or a revelation. You recall that Joseph maintained a close relationship with God from a young age; he abstained from all appearances of evil and refused to join his brothers in doing wrong while on the field; instead, he exposed them. Even in deep trouble in Potiphar's house, he maintained his relationship with God; in prison, he was closer to God than ever. His intimacy with God defined his dreams.

I gave an example of that schoolboy, Jerry, earlier dreamt about what he preoccupied his mind with during the day. Football defined his dreams. The same applies to those preoccupied with God; you'll keep seeing Him and more of Him in your dreams. God will deliberately ensure you're not in darkness concerning essential issues of the kingdom. You must understand that dreams are the mental picture of your future. It helps you picture things foreword and grasp vividly the reality of what's yet to come as though it's natural to you.

God gives unique gifts and abilities to men to carry out specific spiritual assignments. 1 Corinthians 12 explains a lot of these special abilities. Although interpretations of dreams are not mentioned in 1 Corinthians 12, we know that interpretation is from God, said Joseph. Virtually every human can hear from God through dreams, but only a few can explore this as Joseph did. How accurate are your dreams? How often do you get strong messages from God through your dreams? How transparent are your dreams when you have them? Are you able to interpret them? Or do you fret like Pharaoh when you dream?

Your ability to have quality dreams, dreams that are of God, dreams that are revelations, is a direct function of your intimacy with God. Joseph was more than a dreamer; even Pharaoh could dream. What differentiates you from others is being more than a dreamer. For Joseph, he dreams and interprets dreams; he could turn his dreams into realities. He knew when a dream was a vision; he was a dream analyzer to those around him. That's what the Spirit of God can make of anyone who cares to know God more profound than ever. God gives you the grace to see more profound than the dream. I pray that God will quicken your dream life and help you come alive in the Spirit in Jesus' name.

Chapter 8

JOSEPH LIFTED FROM PRISON TO THE PALACE

Genesis 41: 8 – 35

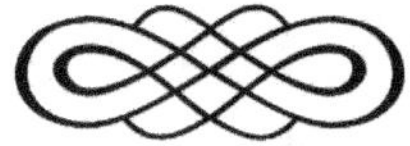

Divine Elevation will bring the best out of us and make us a blessing to others. Promotion will make us grow and become mature in serving God through advancement. **Fitzgerald Odonkor**

I earnestly pray to God for you and me to raise, lift, ad increase us to a height we never dreamed of. The beautiful thing about this prayer is that it is already answered in Ephesians 3:20 "Now to him who can do immeasurably more than all we ask or imagine, according to his power that is at work within us." God wants every one of His children to share in a promotion or lifting since it is a gift from Him. In any event, the test is that many people dislike heavenly lifting more than they ought to, and when a few people do, they need help handling it. Given the state of things, the mystery of divine lifting lasts a lifetime. The vital elements that will make it possible are provided in this book.

This section will examine how Joseph was lifted from Prison to the palace. Was it a mere coincidence? Was it a divinely orchestrated plan? Was there any input on your side of Joseph? How exactly was he lifted? Can one be removed from Prison and be made a prime minister just like that? Did he undergo training before the time that qualifies him for this position? How did this happen? Imagine that Joseph did not fumble.

These and many more will be discussed as we move on in this section. We shall see how good relationships paid off in the long run, how Joseph became a problem solver in his World, and how he demonstrated the wisdom of God in proffering to a challenge that was yet to come. Let's see more!

The World needs Solutions.

When you read the news today, our World is plagued with several dangerous challenges, ranging from Sin, Unbelief, Armed Conflict, Chronic Diseases, Education, Infectious Diseases, Population Growth, Biodiversity, Climate Change, Hunger, Malnutrition, Natural Disasters, Water and Sanitation and many more.

World leaders occasionally gather for a lasting solution to our decaying World. Although, there isn't anything lasting anyone can do to ultimately save the World as it is built to fade away according to the scriptures. This could result from the sinful nature that has permeated the whole creation. This is why everything in this World is produced to expire or depreciate; nothing lasts forever except God's Word. The Bible says, "Heaven and earth will pass away, but not a dot of my Word will pass away" (Matthew 24:35). So the issues on climate change, viruses, and many challenging circumstances that are cropping every day are a sign of how imminent the return of the master is; however, the World is in immediate need of solutions to these challenges.

Can you imagine a Christian coming up with a promising vaccine to HIV or any of the pandemics; can you imagine a Christian inventing a tech solution to climate change to save the ozone layer from wearing away, and can you imagine a child of God coming with an invention by the Spirit of God that can change somethings in this World. So, don't you think we are underutilizing the Spirit of God in us? Our God is creative, and He released his creative ability in a man right from creation when He released His breath on man. That was His image, His real nature, the ability to create. So, it is possible to carry God in you, and you're not positively impacting your World.

Joseph understood this and took full advantage of it. He solved a national problem. See, the magnitude of the solution you proffer determines the kind of people you attract or the kind of attention you get. The scripture says, "A man's gift makes way for him...." Proverbs 18:16. Joseph was a solution-giver. He did not run away from challenges; he faced them as they came and provided appropriate solutions. What are you doing in your small corner? Do you only speak in tongues with nothing to show for it? Have you shown Christ in that small corner of yours?

Let's also be reminded of Daniel and the other three Hebrew brethren. The scriptures tell us that they had an excellent spirit, were rich in wisdom, understood science, and understood deep spiritual mysteries that they could interpret dreams and analyze visions. They were good academically and also sounded spiritual. That was the kind of life Joseph lived. This should be our testimony today too!

The truth is, there's no limit to which the Spirit of God can help us do great things in this World. We can change our World in all aspects as enabled by the Spirit of God. So, let's see a scripture that will unfold what we are discussing here.

"And it came to pass in the morning that his spirit was troubled, and he sent and called for all the magicians of Egypt, and all the wise men thereof: and Pharaoh told them his dream, but there was none that could interpret them unto Pharaoh." Genesis 41:8

In the previous chapter, we looked at the type of dream Pharaoh had, and I wouldn't want to go back to it here. But I want us to know that at this point, the king was troubled and needed solace, and the only way he could get that was to find answers to his dreams. Pharaoh sent his magicians to interpret his dreams, but they needed help. This troubled Pharaoh the more! You see, this was a national issue. Every President, King, or leader has dreams of some sought for the people they lead and needs people to interpret these dreams. Any of these leaders are still looking for those to help them solve their dreams/visions/aspirations differently. Do you have a solution at hand for such dreams if asked now? So, what happened next with the king's dreams which were urgent to be interpreted? It is important to note something important here. In the same way, Pharaoh lacked help from his dream experts. It is also possible not to find all that we need, however urgent, by seeking the World's ways and methods.[4]

Good Relationship Eventually Produced Dividends

"Then spoke the chief butler unto Pharaoh, saying, I do remember my faults this day: Pharaoh was wroth with his servants and put me in ward in the captain of the guard's house, both me and the chief baker: and we dreamed a dream in one night, I and he; we dreamed each man according to the interpretation of his dream. And there was a young man, and Hebrew, servant to the captain of the guard; and we told him, and he interpreted our dreams; to each man according to his dream, he did interpret. And it came to pass, as he interpreted to us, so it was; me he restored unto mine office, and him he hanged." Genesis 41:9-13.

I love how the chief butler started the discussion and admitted to having failed Joseph. He was the only person that knew Joseph's true story; how he was brought to Egypt as an enslaved person and how his master's wife lied against him. Of course, the butler wouldn't want to say a word to anybody because of fear, but at this point, he had no option but to suggest Joseph to the king.

This was more like when they needed someone to play the guitar for Saul at the palace; David was suggested. But, again, something must link you to the palace or a more significant opportunity. What do you have that can connect you to such? The bottom line is how Joseph's good relationship in the Prison eventually paid off. The care Joseph showed to the butler was never

---

[4] Matt Erickson, *The Life of Joseph: God's Sovereignty in Our Suffering*, A Lenten Devotional (Eastbrook Church, n.d.), 31, www.eastbrook.org.

in vain. Now, there was a need that only Joseph could supply. This was very strategic. The only person with the solution is in Prison; even those who have forgotten him suddenly remember him.

You must understand that for your dream to be interpreted, you must also help interpret other people's dreams because it is interwoven with their dreams. Joseph interpreted the butler's dream, and now the butler has to help to interpret Joseph's dream, a dream he has had since he was seventeen years old. Don't joke with strategic relationships; God can put them around you to help you soar. After high school, I wanted to train in theology and serve in the church. However, I was bogged down by my lack of faith in God's provision. In his ways, God brought Rev. Walter Rutto, the AGC Missionary, to Turkana. He discovered I was passionate about serving God in full-time ministry and badly desired to train for the same. God used him as my strategic partner in leading me to the place I earnestly needed to help me be equipped for God's service in the church. He told me one afternoon in his house, "Paul, AGC has a bible college in Kericho. We will trust God to lead you through this if you are interested. Apply, and I will take the forms, for I am traveling home soon." Those strategic words became the seed for my training and serving God in full-time ministry. God can be able to do the same for you today.

Unprecedented Exit from Prison

"Then Pharaoh sent and called Joseph, and they hastily brought him out of the dungeon: he shaved, changed his raiment, and came unto Pharaoh. And Pharaoh said unto Joseph, I have dreamed a dream, and none can interpret it: and I have heard say of thee, that thou canst understand a dream to interpret it." Genesis 41:14-15

Sometimes, this story may look so simple; is it effortless to get out a man charged with attempted rape? But, of course, offenses like that, before the law, and the caliber of the person Joseph offended (so to speak) isn't just any person but an eminent personality. So, to get out of Prison required intervention of divinity.

So, it was unprecedented the way Joseph came out of Prison. He left the Prison in the most unlikely way anyone could think. And at this point, he was dealing directly with the highest authority of the land. The white house already declared that he be brought out of Prison; can anyone else return him there? Can Potiphar, who threw him there, say otherwise? When a king declares a thing in a kingdom, it's final. So now Joseph was out of the Prison unprecedentedly, and his freedom was now in his hand to interpret the dreams and remain free or to interpret the visions and return to the Prison. But there was a gift in Joseph that cannot but manifest. Hallelujah!

The Gift of Interpretation in Action

No man can do anything except God helps him. God is the giver of gifts, but it has to do with man's cooperation to allow them to manifest fully. No doubt Joseph had the advantage of the interpretation of dreams. This is far from the use of indications and occurrences. If you see in your dreams, it indicates that you are slow in life. Well, for Joseph, it was more profound than just telling him his dream. He interprets based on what God is saying through the dream.

Let's look at what Joseph himself said;

*"And Joseph answered Pharaoh, saying, **it is not in me: God shall give Pharaoh an answer of peace."*** Genesis 41:16

The reply of Joseph here says it all; God interprets our dreams, not man. God is the giver of the gift of understanding. God still gives gifts to men, and He gives us these gifts to profit us and the body of Christ. The gifts are meant to promote us and position us for greatness. The question is, what do you do with the gifts of God in your life?

Joseph gave the king a very accurate interpretation of his dreams by the Spirit of God, and the king was dazed at the kind of human being Joseph was. The message of the two dreams was profound; it takes only a spiritually inclined person to unravel the mystery behind the dreams. No wonder the magicians and others couldn't interpret the dreams.

The Spirit of God in us is meant to help us fulfill divine mandate in every aspect of human endeavors. Therefore, we must rise to the occasion whenever the opportunity comes to manifest the image of God in us. God is still counting on us. Are you there for Him? Can God trust you with critical spiritual abilities? Can you be an answer to the yearnings of your people? Is there a gift in you that can save the unborn generation? They are tough questions to answer but worthy of effort because they are deep and foundational in our being for greatness.

Pharaoh Attested to the Presence of God upon Joseph

"Now, therefore, let Pharaoh look out a man discreet and wise and set him over the land of Egypt. Let Pharaoh do this, and let him appoint officers over the ground, and take up the fifth part of the land of Egypt in the seven plenteous years. And let them gather all the food of those good years that come, lay up corn under the hand of Pharaoh, and let them keep food in the cities. And that food shall be stored to the land against the seven years of famine, which shall be in the land of Egypt; that the land perishes not through the famine. And the thing was good in the eyes of Pharaoh, and in the eyes of all his servants. **And Pharaoh said unto his servants, can we find such unmanned as this whom the Spirit of God is?** Genesis 41:33-38

Joseph had now interpreted Pharaoh's dreams as an impending famine and the possible way to avert it or escape starvation. But he didn't just stop there; he suggested a way out with a detailed analysis of how it should be done. King Pharaoh could not but attest that the Spirit of God was with Joseph, as seen in the last statement above.

After Joseph suggested that the king should look out for someone in the kingdom, who is trustworthy and prudent to entrust with the assignment of storing up food for the first seven years, the king replied Joseph by saying; *"Can we find someone as good as Joseph in the kingdom, a man in whom the Spirit of God is?"* Wow! Can there be times when our bosses at work will attest to the Spirit of God in our life? Can those around you testify that God is working through you? This attestation indeed yielded fruits for Joseph. The king said no one else has this kind of Spirit and wisdom. So, the king was already suggesting that if we must get someone to do this, it has to be you!

Divine Promotion

"And Pharaoh said unto Joseph, forasmuch as God hath showed thee all this, there is none as discreet and wise as thou art: thou shall be over my house, and according unto thy word shall all my people be ruled: only in the throne will I be greater than thou. And Pharaoh said unto Joseph, I have set thee over all the land of Egypt. And Pharaoh took off his ring from his hand, put it upon Joseph's hand, arrayed him in fine linen vestures, and put a gold chain about his neck, and made him ride in the second chariot which he had. They cried before him, bowed their knees made him ruler over all the land of Egypt. And Pharaoh said unto Joseph, I am Pharaoh, and without thee shall no man lift hand foot in all the land of Egypt." Genesis 41:39-45

Indeed, promotion only comes from God. Who would've thought Joseph would be out of Prison before this time to talk of becoming a prime minister? No one saw it coming! But God always has His agenda.

This immediately confirmed Joseph as the Prime Minister before anyone who was probably handling the position before Joseph came out of Prison. It was like a movie; a few minutes ago, he became a prisoner and a prime minister a few minutes later. This is miraculous! I call this "P2P" (Prison to Palace). Only God can promote a man like that. But, of course, the king couldn't have done this without divine orchestration.

Who says you can't get up there? Who says your prison experience will end your life? Who says you can't be promoted from Prison to the palace? Who are they that say a thing, and it comes to pass when God has not spoken?

Joseph's brothers intended to end his dreams. Hence, they said, let's kill him and see what will become of his dreams. But can you kill God's plan in anyone's life? I wonder what is going through their mind of Joseph at this junction; it seems like he was dreaming. He would say to himself, "Is this me?" Indeed, when the Lord turns the captivity of Zion again, we become like them in that dream. What a promotion for Joseph! Finally, Joseph sees his dream come to light.

Light at the End of the Tunnel

What a turnaround! Joseph became a prime minister in a foreign land. When you read Genesis 41 from 46-57, you realize that Joseph became great, blessed with a wife and lovely children. Remember, he came to Egypt as an enslaved person, but God turned things. God will turn things around for you in Jesus's name. Amen! Know this; no matter how the devil tries to manipulate or delay your destiny, it can't stop you. God is on His throne. It doesn't matter how long the enemy has kept you on the dark side of your destiny, no matter how tough it; has been, no matter the number of years you've spent in Prison, no matter the deprivations, no matter the setups, no matter the attacks, have in mind; God is on His throne. There will always be light at the end of the tunnel. But would you trust God as Joseph did? Would you please God as Joseph did? Will you do the will of God, even in pain, as Joseph did? Would you choose to do the right even if it means death? Can you stand out for God when everyone is involved in evil?

Joseph stood out, and the result was glorious. If you genuinely desire the glory of Joseph as a prime minister, you must do what he did. There is no cheap success. Every success comes with a price. Are you ready to pay the fee?

Chapter 9

JOSEPH AT WORK

Genesis 41:46-57

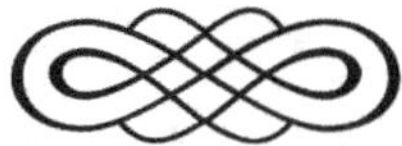

The only way to do great work is to love what you do. If you haven't found it yet, keep looking. Don't settle." **Steve Jobs**

Joseph's Wise Plan

Joseph had the right stuff of good administration. Joseph was directed by God and thus ready to design cautiously and anticipate what would probably occur. But, to do his unmistakable preparation, he needed to be empowered to do the work. Anybody responsible for such an enormous task requires the power to pursue and complete speedy choices that others will regard and comply with.

Joseph's arrangement appeared great to Pharaoh and his authorities (Genesis 41:37). The nearby administration acknowledged and confided in his arrangements. As a result, Joseph had the trust of a multitude of individuals. In crisis circumstances, there should be that confidence in the administration. Individuals are under extraordinary strain and need a pioneer they can trust.

Joseph quickly approached the work to which Pharaoh had delegated him. His vital interest was caring for other people's business instead of exploiting his new situation at the top of the illustrious court. He kept up with his confidence in God, giving his kids names that acknowledged God for mending him close to home agony and making him productive (Gen. 41:51-52). He perceived that his insight and wisdom were gifts from God; however, he had much to learn about where he was - Egypt, its rural industry specifically.

As the senior overseer, Joseph's work addressed every down-to-earth region of the country. His office would have expected that he would find out a lot about regulation, correspondence, discussion, transportation, protected and productive techniques for food capacity, building, monetary planning and estimating, record-keeping, finance, the treatment of exchanges both through cash and through bargaining, HR, and the obtaining of land. His remarkable capacities, as given by God, were a special gift to the people in Egypt and beyond. The virtuoso of Joseph's prosperity lay in the successful coordination of his heavenly skills and obtained capabilities. For Joseph, this was all original work. The ability that God gave Joseph was phenomenal. It is true that not all about Joseph was written in the Bible, and so we can presume that the life of Joseph was full of many experiences that God utilized to bring him where he came to unravel the greatness that God had built in him.

Sometimes in the intense moments of obscure life and training, you may not know how God can use your expertise and experience. However, that may not be our business, but to do our best at any given moment and trust Him for the next steps of life since He is always omnipresent (ever-present), omnipotent (all-powerful), and omniscient (all-knowing). The good thing is that with all these abilities and capabilities, something will be remembered. However minute it may be. This is because he cares so much that he understands the usefulness of His creatures at all times.

One-fifth of the gather was taken from the rancher for food save. Joseph fostered another example of land use. In his book *Biblical Principles of Building Wealth, Ainsley Reid* speaks of one-fifth (20%) as one of the very principles in God's word for anyone to get wealthy. According to him, if you save 20% of your income, the power of compound interest will take place over time, and you will eventually reap great wealth in the long run—a great lesson for us today.

Certain things created in a crisis can become typical examples of how the grain was put away and disseminated spread the work and obligation throughout the country. Rather than having one colossal focus, Joseph urged every district to set up stockrooms.

Egypt was the mainland that was ready for starvation in the Center East. It addressed its issues as well as those of adjoining nations. Great fiasco arranging can have broad advantages. No sign was given that this dry spell was a judgment from God on Pharaoh and Egypt. On the contrary, it has been a characteristic catastrophe. Be that as it may, God utilized the calamity alleviation undertaking to save Jacob's family and the future country of Israel. God can use disaster arrangements to accomplish something worthwhile and accomplish his motivations on the planet. And the same applies to other challenges that come in life. Something could be harmful in your sight and imagination, but God could be working on something to achieve His purposes which are usually excellent and beneficial to His creatures. You may never understand God in such occurrences, but you can trust Him to lead you through an extraordinary path beautifully orchestrated for your greater good.

Management Skills from Joseph

1. Joseph had Foresight

Joseph received some unique wisdom from God about the coming crisis. But we need to learn through personal experience and observing other people's lives that a financial crisis could be just around the corner. We don't need a midnight dream to know that a broken furnace, a hospital visit, or a lost job will happen someday. Therefore, we should develop a financial plan to manage the issue before the crisis begins because we know this. Foresight is needed in every area of life, without which we get into enormous challenges that cost our lives.

2. Joseph Was Honest

When faced with the news, Joseph was upfront with Pharaoh about the depth of the crisis. He didn't sugar-coat it or make it seem less important than it was. People were going to die — that that's a pretty tough pill to swallow. The severity of the issue was never in question. With this knowledge, they took the proper steps to solve it. Joseph told Pharaoh what was true, and that saved the situation. The truth will always set us free.

3. Joseph was a Sacrificial Leader

Human tendency is to live it up during the good times. The concept of sacrifice runs counter to our nature when everything runs smoothly. We'd rather spend in the present than save money for the future. If Joseph and the rest of Egypt had followed the "live-it-up" path, they would have perished when the famine hit. Instead, they sacrificed during the time of plenty to save themselves from the future financial crisis. Sacrifice is a virtue to be highly esteemed because every sacrifice counts and is rewarded at the right time. Sometimes it is good to obey God, and sometimes the flow of things.

I remember when I was in primary school, and life was tough. There were many voices, including that of quitting. However, I knew education was the key to my next step to victory. Despite the challenges I faced, I found myself encouraged by the fact that my success in education was also an eye-opener for my family. I made many sacrifices during those years to make it to High school. Every young man can achieve much in life if willing to go the extra mile by sacrificing for the greater good.

4. Joseph understood Business and Savings

How did they sacrifice? Joseph instructed the Egyptians to save 20% of the produce from the land each year. They took to that task for seven years, putting the grain in storage bins. Joseph's passion for saving can be seen in his never stopping. He wasn't taking any chances. The Bible tells us that he collected so much grain that he couldn't count it anymore and stopped keeping records (Gen. 41:49). That's an intense stockpile, more than enough to meet the need.

5. Joseph made the food accessible.

All this grain was placed in storehouses near the cities. He didn't ship the grain to some remote location where he needed to get to it at the right time. He didn't convert or trade the grain into a non-liquid asset like land or precious jewels. Those would have been useless in a food crisis. Instead, he knew this resource would be needed in a relatively short time frame, so he kept the food in its current condition and as accessible as possible.

6. Joseph was a disciplined Leader.

The planning for and living through this crisis period lasted 14 years. I'm sure at some point during the years of plenty, certain Egyptians scoffed at the preparations that were taking place. However, Joseph stayed faithful to his task with intense focus and discipline. He never wavered or allowed distractions to sway his commitment to saving the people. And finally, everyone was happy that they had a focused leader.

Chapter 10

JOSEPH TEACHES – 'YOUR SIN WILL FIND YOU OUT

Genesis 42: 1 – 43:14

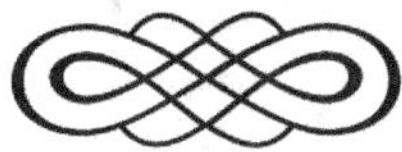

But if you fail to do this, you will sin against the Lord; you may be sure that your sin will find you out. **Numbers 32:23 NIV**

Every action on earth has a resultant effect. Indeed, to every effort, there's an equal and opposite reaction. Nothing happens in this world without a cause. If there's smoke somewhere, be sure to see fire around the smoke. Every success you see is a function of an effort from someone; also, every failure you see is a function of someone's negligence. The entire life revolves around actions and results. No action goes unrewarded either by humans or by the act itself. This is the very reason why we must be careful of the activities we display.

Jane aborted three good times because she felt Brian wasn't rich enough to have a child with; the first time was a mutual agreement between her and Brian, but the second time was her decision against Brian's. The last time they resulted in their separation. Years later, Jane was born again, as well as Brian. Timothy, Brian's cousin, decided to come home with his fiancée after spending a long time working in the UK. On arriving in Canada, their home country, he excitedly called Brian to make every necessary arrangement for the reception of his wife-to-be. The entire family was gathered in anticipation of the girl, faces full of smiles. The moment they were all waiting for was finally here; all eyes were on the door as the living room was full of family members. The little ones in the house would come into the living room to ask, "Grandma, when is she arriving?" It was more like a queen would be received in the family.

Finally, the moment came, the car horn to the alert, and all eyes were on the compound gate as Timothy and the lady came out of the vehicle. They immediately entered the living room, where the family members were waiting. As she walked in, they all screamed, expressing their emotions. Timothy felt so happy to see his family welcome her, not knowing some of the shouts were adverse reactions.

Soon they all calmed down, and Brian walked out of the room with his sister, who ran to the room to call Brian. Although both went straight to the girl with unhappy facial expressions, the room's atmosphere changed immediately as the family saw a connection between Brian and the lady. Then Brian said; Jane, what are you doing here? Do you know each other? Timothy asked. Yes, of course; replied Brian. This was the same girl I told you about some time ago. This girl killed my babies and decided to live with other guys she felt could sleep with her. Timothy, I think you just miscalculated your steps and need to retrace your steps. You haven't found a wife. Timothy was devastated and eventually called off the relationship, having heard that from Brian. Although Jane was now born again, somehow, what she did a couple of years ago hurt her. Beloved, you must be mindful of what you do in life.

The Reality of the Prevailing Famine

Joseph's brothers did the same thing to Joseph. They started committing evil long before they sold out Joseph. They hated Joseph for dreaming; they harbored evil against him and plotted to kill him for no reason. They wanted to kill were it not for God's intervention. And the Lord lifted Joseph afterward to become the prime minister of Egypt.

In Genesis 42, the Bible tells us that the anticipated famine eventually started, and it hit most of the countries around Egypt, including Canaan. So, Jacob decided to send his children to get some food for the family in Egypt. They had an excellent ride to Egypt, where they intended to buy food. They would have escaped the famine if Joseph had still lived with them. Do you know why? God should have told them ahead through Joseph so they could run. But they were caught unaware because there was no spiritual guide. No one among them could see into the future. The only one who had that ability was sold out for jealousy. What a world! What do you think will happen to them in Egypt?

Joseph's First Dream Fulfilled

"And Joseph was the governor over the land, and he it was that sold to all the people of the land: **Joseph's brethren came, and bowed down before him with their faces to the earth.** *And Joseph saw his brethren, and he knew them, but made himself strange unto them, and spoke roughly unto them; and he said unto them, whence come ye? And they said, from the land of Canaan to buy food. And Joseph knew his brethren, but they knew not him."* Genesis 42:6-9.

What do you see in the highlighted bolded part of the verses above? For me, I see a fulfillment of Joseph's first dream; the sheaves of his brothers finally bowing down to Joseph's sheaf. His brothers arrived in Egypt and never knew Joseph was in charge of the food as the new prime minister. So, when they appeared before him, they bowed down to the ground in homage to the power without knowing it was Joseph. They bowed before him exactly the way he saw it in his dream.

Sometimes we abandon our dreams because of opposition. Joseph had a plan at age seventeen, and the fulfillment came 13 years later. It was 13 years of ups and downs, but the Lord turned it for good. Here you have his brothers bowing down before him, the same people that sold him out.

The question is, what would you do if you were Joseph? Pause to think about that for a while.

A Display of Wisdom

"And he said unto them, nay, but to see the nakedness of the land ye come. And they said.............. And Joseph said unto them, that is it that I spoke unto you, saying, ye are spies: at this moment ye shall be at this moment: by the life of Pharaoh ye shall not go forth hence, except your youngest brother hither.

SendTherefore, sendoff you and let him fetch your brother, and ye shall be kept in prison................. And Joseph said unto them the third day, this do, and live; for I fear God: if ye be true men, let one of your brethren be bound in the house of your prison: go ye, carry corn for the famine of your houses: but bring your youngest brother unto me; so, shall your words be verified, and ye shall not die. And they did so." Genesis 42:12-20

Some may think Joseph was giving them a tough time to make them feel pain. I believe that wasn't the case. Joseph needed to verify the genuineness of their claims. You can imagine them saying to Joseph that Joseph was dead. Joseph knew they were lying because he was standing right before them. In his heart, he'll say I'm not dead; I'm standing here before you. Joseph also tried to confirm without a shadow that his brother (Benjamin) was still alive. He must have missed his brother so much and would want to be if they did not harm him as they did to him. Joseph had to use every method possible to make sure Benjamin was alive. That shows how caring Joseph was. Though he was away, he had his brother in mind.

He had to retain one of them to compel them to bring Benjamin along when coming next. This was tough for them, but they hadn't any option but to do it. What a pain for Reuben to bear!

The Torture of Guilt

You can begin to imagine what Joseph's brother was going through. Gradually, nemesis was catching up with them. Let's look at what happened next and learn a few lessons from it.

"And they said one to another, we are verily guilty concerning our brother, in that we saw the anguish of his soul when he besought us, and we would not hear; therefore, is this distress come upon us. And Reuben answered them,

saying, " I not unto you, do not sin against the child; and ye would not hear? Therefore, behold, also his blood is required. And they knew not that Joseph understood them; for he spoke unto them by an interpreter." Genesis 42:21-23

This passage reveals how cruel they were to Joseph; He begged them with tears not to harm him, but they wouldn't listen. Then, finally, they remembered how evil they were to Joseph and all that transpired, and they began to feel guilty. They said one to another; maybe it's a sin we committed against our brother that is catching up on us now; indeed, it was. They were in a mess because of what they did tens of years ago.

The torture got worst as Joseph instructed that their sacks be filled with food and that their money be returned to their bags without their knowledge. They got to the road and discovered they had their money back. Everyone had his money returned to his bag; they became terrified, unaware of what was happening. What torture! Take a look at the verse below;

"And he said unto his brethren, my money is restored; and, lo, it is even in my sack: and **their heart failed them, and they were afraid, saying one to another, what is this that God hath done unto us?"** Genesis 42:28

The fact that their heart failed them is what caught my attention here. They became so afraid that they felt pain in their hearts. The torture was much. Suddenly they realized that God was dealing with them because of their past errors. This is important; they are beginning to admit their mistakes, but was it too late? They've retained one of them in Egypt, and now they've discovered their money has been returned to their bags; the thought of how to convince their father to allow Benjamin to go with them is also there, a couple of challenging issues at the same time. Is this pain not too much?

They were hard-hearted when they did everything they did to Joseph; they never knew a day like this would come. It was time for them to feel the pain as well. No wonder the Bible says, "Be not deceived, God is not mocked; for whatever a man sows, that he will also reap" (Galatians 6:7). Know this, what you do today can come to hurt you tens of years later. You must be careful what you do today.

Jacob's Grieve: A Chain Effect

One essential thing in this world is that every error committed always has chain effects. For example, sometimes, a father makes a mistake, affecting the children years later. In this case, the children messed up, and the father got affected by the children's actions.

"And Jacob their father said unto them, I have ye bereaved of my children: Joseph is not, and Simeon is not, and ye will take Benjamin away: all these things are against me.........And he said, My son shall not go down with you; for his brother is dead, and he is left alone: if mischief befalls him by the way in the which ye go, then shall ye bring down my grey hairs with sorrow to the grave." Genesis 42:36-38

Jacob wept and would not be comforted; Joseph was gone, Simeon was taken hostage, and Benjamin was to be taken away from him again. It was indeed a pathetic situation. He cried and refused to let them go with Benjamin. But for how long will you leave Simeon hostage?

A Prayer of Mercy

Jacob had refused to let Reuben and his brother take Benjamin along to Egypt, but as we see in chapter 43, verses 1-13, the famine got so tensed and prolonged that the food they bought from Egypt earlier was finished, and they needed to go back for more. Again, the reality of facing Joseph was done to them. They had abandoned Simeon there for quite a while, but at this time, they had to return. Would Jacob let them go with Benjamin? Reuben had to plead with their father, again and again, to let him go with Benjamin. Finally, Jacob queried why they had to tell the prime minister they had another brother at home. Eventually, Jacob lets Benjamin go with them. But before letting them go, he did something so significant; he gave them very costly advice and prayed that God would have mercy on them, precisely what they needed the most at that time.

"And their father Israel said unto them, If it must be so now, do this; take of the best fruits in the land in your vessels, and carry down the man a present, a little balm, and a little honey, spices, and myrrh, nuts, and almonds: And take double money in your hand; and the money that was brought again in the mouth of your sacks, carry it again in your hand; peradventure it was an oversight: also take your brother, and arise, go again unto the man: **and God Almighty give you mercy before the man, that he may send away your other brother and Benjamin.** *If I am bereaved of my children, I am bereaved."* Genesis 43:11-14.

All they needed at this point was the mercy of God. They prayed that God would touch the prime minister, whom they never knew was their brother, to understand them. The same people who sold out Joseph were at his mercy. Jacob asked God for mercy for his children. How often do you pray to God to understand your children? How often do you ask for mercy for yourself when you see you've gone wrong? Well, they messed up big time, they went too far, but God's still merciful no matter how we've gone into errors. May the Lord also have mercy on you in Jesus' name.

Chapter 11

JOSEPH TEACHES –
FORGIVE AND REVENGE, NOT

Genesis 43: 15 – 16; 45: 1 – 5

There is no revenge so complete as forgiveness. **Josh Billings**

Forgiveness is a spirit, and unforgiveness is also a spirit. What determines your operation at any given time is the spirit that possesses you. The natural man tends to manifest the latter (unforgiveness) easily. On the other hand, the Adamic nature in man enjoys harboring things and keeping records of wrongs. This is why people naturally retaliate when hurt; even those born again are equally tempted sometimes to fire back at people.

The elements of unforgiveness are bitterness, anger, ego, and pride. These elements make us keep looking backward instead of going foreword. Do you know? Hatred hurts the hater more than the hated. It pays to forgive than to hold on to past hurts and occurrences. The scripture warns us to forgive before praying to God in Mark 11:25-26. Our heavenly Father will not forgive us if we do not forgive. Jesus also taught His disciples to ask God to forgive their trespasses as they also forgive those who have wronged them. You can't ask God to forgive when you're still harboring so much against your neighbor. It doesn't work like that!

Some of us will say, sir, what this guy did to me is unheard. Can you imagine he lied against me, and I got sacked from the office? Another person will say, he kept me waiting until the dying minute, when I had no suitors again before he called off the wedding, and you ask me to forgive him? Someone else will say I employed this so-called brother and entrusted him with my business. Still, he embezzled my money, wreaked havoc on my business, and ran away. Should I still forgive him? The list is endless, but shouldn't you forgive?

Beloved, I share in your pain, but you have to forgive. Take a clue from the life of Joseph; would you forgive your brothers if you were in Joseph's shoes? Indeed, it takes the spirit of forgiveness to forgive genuinely. In this section, we shall learn from the life of Joseph how he forgave his brothers and every other person that offended him despite all they did to him.

Joseph Forgave Potiphar's Wife

Interestingly, the bible is silent about what happened to Potiphar and his wife after Joseph became the prime minister. Have you ever asked how Potiphar's wife felt when Joseph eventually became the Prime Minister? How would they stand before Joseph? What will be going through their minds, especially the woman?

Joseph spent many years in prison because of the woman's lies; he was confined for years for what he didn't do. And now, he's in power. So, what would you do if you were Joseph?

From a close look at the scriptures, Joseph did not retaliate; he forgave Potiphar's wife. Otherwise, the scriptures should've recorded it if he later punished them. It's possible they apologized to him, but the bottom line is that he forgave her. Likewise, Joseph didn't mention it in the king's hearing; instead, he kept mute to cover up not to attract the king's wrath on them. This is true forgiveness, forgiveness orchestrated by the Spirit of God.

Not Revenge

Some would look at the emotional stress Joseph made his brothers go through and think it was some revenge. However, the actions here are far from revenge; it was a mere precaution to help the situation.

"And the men took that present, and they took double money in their hand, and Benjamin rose, down to Egypt, and stood before Joseph. And when Joseph saw Benjamin with them, he said to the ruler of his house, bring these men home, slay, and make ready; for these men shall dine with me at noon." Genesis 43:15-16

Reuben set out and headed for Egypt with Benjamin and his other brothers. And when Joseph saw Benjamin with them, he was happy and ordered his servants to prepare special meat so he could dine and wine with his brothers. The remaining part of chapter 43 explains how they were afraid as they walked towards Joseph's house; one of them drew near to one of Joseph's offices and said,

"See, when we came the last time, we discovered you returned our money to our bags while we were on our way home. But we have come back with it and many more." He said that because they thought Joseph was seeking an occasion against them because of the money.

They were given water to wash their feet as they were about to get into Joseph's house. The treatment at this point was becoming suspicious, yet none of them could say this was it. I guess they were ready for whatever came on them. Finally, in chapter 44, Joseph entered as the table was set to dine. Benjamin was served more food and meat than the rest of them. While eating, Joseph asked their Father, "How about your aged Dad? Is he still alive?" They replied yes, he was alive, and that he was doing well too.

Again, Joseph instructed his servants to fill their bags with food, as much as they could carry. He also told them to insert his silver cup in Benjamin's bag without their knowledge. He did this to bring them back as they set out to go. While on their way home, the guards ran after them and indicted them of stealing from the king. They denied it, but after searching, they discovered Benjamin had the king's cup in his bag. They were so afraid that they almost lost their breath. They pleaded with Joseph, who wanted Benjamin to stay with him, but Reuben would disagree based on his promise to his Father; he would rather stay back, even if it meant death than let Benjamin stay back. So, they must take the pain to explain the situation to Joseph and how their old man would die to hear that Benjamin is retained in Egypt.

Joseph Reveals his Identity and Forgives his Brothers

Just think about the emotional pain Joseph's brother went through here. Some of them thought; this is it; we're dead today! I guess they already gave up on life at this point. This is what happens when we give our hearts to do evil. True, every sin we commit returns to hurt in the future. This was, again, a substantial emotional torture for Joseph's brothers. And at this point, Joseph was already suffering from within. He tried to control it the first time as he went to cry in his room, washed his face, and returned to them, but at some point, he could not refrain like a baby; he immediately ordered all his servants to leave the premises.

In chapter 45, you see that emotion has built up in Joseph and his brothers. Joseph then made himself known to his brothers, and they all wept on each other. Take a look at the verses below as we draw out the lessons here;

"Then Joseph could not refrain before all those that stood by him, and he cried, cause every man to go out from me. And no man stood with him while Joseph made himself known to his brethren. And he wept aloud: the Egyptians and the house of Pharaoh heard. And Joseph said unto his brethren, I am Joseph; doth my Father yet live? And his brethren could not answer him; for they were troubled at his presence. And Joseph said unto his brethren, come near to me, I pray you. And they came near. And he said, I am Joseph your brother, whom ye sold into Egypt. Therefore, be not grieved, nor angry with yourselves, that ye sold me hither: God sent me before you to preserve life." Genesis 45:1-5

Joseph revealing himself to his brothers must have been challenging, as seen from the scriptures above. But when we recollect ourselves and view God in His wisdom and power, we appreciate the words of pastor Jacob even in our situations today. As he said in one of his sermons ", Although God's ways can be difficult to understand at times, it's clear that He uses everyday events and ordinary people to accomplish."[5]

Here is the Real Act of Forgiveness

Joseph wept and called them to come closer. Can you see that? Some of us wouldn't want them to come closer ever again! Some would say, never cross my path; maintain your lane as I keep mine. But Joseph said, "Come closer, don't be afraid that I will pay back evil for evil." Joseph's brothers were terrified. You could see that they could not answer him when he asked if his Father was still alive. They were completely dumbfounded!

Again, Joseph displayed a caring heart; thinking of how they were feeling, he quickly asked them to draw closer. He told them not to be too hard on themselves for selling him out while he was still very young. To Joseph, it was part of God's plan to preserve his people; otherwise, the famine could have wiped Israel from the earth's surface. What a forgiving Spirit!

Many people will not do what Joseph did. We are in a world that revenges in the other of the day. When people get into power, the first thing they do is go after those who offended them centuries ago; isn't that funny? Some make it look like they sought the ability to take revenge on somebody. Joseph never did that. Fine, enemies will always be there, destiny hunters will always come after you, and people will hate you for no reason or even indict you for what you

---

[5] Pastor Jacob, *Joseph and the Gospel of Many Colors*, 2014, 52, www.martinsburgchurch.org/joseph.

know nothing about, as Potiphar's wife did to Joseph; all you need do is forgive, forgive, and forgive.

Will you forgive that man, that woman, that boy, or that girl today?

Chapter 12

JOSEPH: A GENERATIONAL DELIVERER

Genesis 45: 5 – 8; 46- 47; 50: 15 – 21

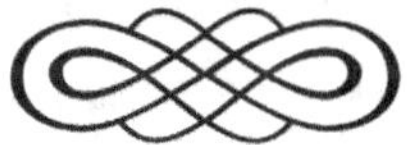

"The primary reason we do too much is that we have never taken the time to discover that portion of what we do that makes the biggest difference." **Andy Stanley, Next Generation Leader: 5 Essentials for Those Who Will Shape the Future**

Just as the world always needs solution providers to its numerous challenges, so do the heavens. God always raises people for specific assignments in every generation. I call them "GENRATIONAL DELIVERERS". Joseph was one of them, Moses was another, Samson was one of them, Gideon, Deborah, Esther, David, Daniel, and so many others made it. These people gave their best to fulfill the will of God in their lives. Some of these guys faced death, while others suffered hardship, but it mattered less as they focused on fulfilling the divine mandate.

Do you aspire to be the Joseph in your family, community, state/county, country, continent, or even the globe? Is there a drive in you to make a difference in this generation? Do you desire greatness in the light of God's word? Let's see through the life of Joseph again in this chapter as we delve deep into the scriptures.

God's Ultimate Agenda is revealed.

"Now, therefore, be not grieved, nor angry with yourselves, that ye sold me hither: God sent me before you to preserve life. For these two years hath the famine been in the land, yet there are five years, in which there shall neither be earing nor harvest. And God sent me before you to preserve your posterity on the earth and to save your lives by a great deliverance. So now it was not you that sent me hither, but God: He has made me a father to Pharaoh, Lord of his entire house, and a ruler throughout all the land of Egypt." Genesis 45:5-8

God allows some things to prove his point. Imagine all that Joseph went through; not even Joseph would've thought he would become a Prime minister in a foreign land. When thrown into the empty well, he would've concluded that he would die there, but God miraculously got him out. In Potiphar's house, he was already getting too used to comfort; meanwhile, Potiphar's house wasn't the actual fulfillment. The place of the assignment was still ahead. God could not afford Joseph to become complacent as he enjoyed freedom in Potiphar's house. There was every tendency for Joseph to decide to relax or settle in Potiphar's house, for he had even become the boss of the house.

God again made his master's wife cast an eye on him. It was all on God's agenda; He knew exactly where he was taking Joseph. Whatever was going to stop Joseph, God would delete. Whenever it was time to upgrade or get promoted, God set up a scenario to move him by force. The critical thing is that Joseph had built a deep personal relationship with God earlier, and he understood the ways of God. I guess Joseph kept seeing God's hand as he journeyed. He could relate to divinely orchestrated circumstances; no wonder he kept pleasing God and maintaining a life of purity even in terrible times. So, it was easy for him to forgive his brother because he knew God was involved. Let's take a look at what Joseph said in Chapter 50.

"And when Joseph's brethren saw that their father was dead, they said, Joseph will peradventure hate us................. And Joseph wept when they spoke unto him. And his brethren also went and fell before his face; and they said, behold, we be thy servants. And Joseph said unto them, fear not: for am I in place of God? But as for you, ye thought evil against me; but God meant it unto pleasing, to bring to pass, as it is this day, to save many people alive. Therefore, fear you not: I will nourish you and your little ones. And he comforted them, and spoke kindly unto them." Genesis 50:15-21

You could see that Joseph knew it was all about God. He told his brother not to bother themselves; it's a fact that their plan was meant for evil, but God made it all good in the end. God sent me ahead of you so we can preserve posterity. God sent me ahead to preserve the covenant He made with Abraham, Isaac, and our father, Jacob. It was God all the way!

It is essential to fulfilling God's purpose for our lives. It helps us stick to him when things look bad; we'll still trust him even in our worst situations. What do you see in your dark moments? Do you know the challenge, or do you see God through the challenge? Do you feel overwhelmed when you think God isn't with you again? Joseph knew God was involved; he kept the vision alive, ensuring life's challenges did not abort it. How do you handle it whenever God takes you through longer routes? Do you stylishly try to avoid the way God wants you to go? Think about that!

Joseph Saved His Family

Upon hearing that Joseph was alive and desired to relocate to Egypt, Jacob inquired of God. This is because; he had a tradition of worship. He set up an altar, made sacrifices, and worshipped God. Afterward, the Lord told him to go down with the children to Egypt. Why must he need God to convince him to go when he was told his son was the prime minister?

The reason isn't farfetched; God had promised them the land of Canaan earlier; living Canaan to Egypt is a deviation from divine order, but God needed to assure him that He was involved (Genesis 46:1-4). God told him, I will make you outstanding in Egypt, and at the right time, I will bring you out again. He needed this assurance to know he was on course. He understood that it's not every open door a man should walk through. Some open doors are traps. Hence, he took time to inquire of the Lord. Joseph's family arrived in Egypt like they were celebrities. But, of course, they were because of Joseph's position. So, the whole land welcomed them. Joseph then went ahead to speak of his family to the king.

"Then Joseph came and told Pharaoh, and said, my father and my brethren, and their flocks, and their herds, and all that they have, are come out of the land of Canaan; and, behold, they are in the land of Goshen." Genesis 47:1

Now they have an influential figure who could speak for them; their status changed. This is what it means to have an eminent personality. Joseph said Israel ensured they had an excellent place to settle and continue their nomadic farming. Indeed, he had become a generational Savior.

A Goshen in Egypt

"And Israel dwelt in the land of Egypt, in the country of Goshen; and they had possessions therein, and grew, and multiplied exceedingly." Genesis 47:27

Goshen was a land full of pasture and vegetation, a region with water suitable for agriculture. Joseph ensured he used his influence to secure the land for his family. As a result, Israel dwelt there with his entire family and flourished as God promised them.

While famine ravaged the other part of the world, Israel secured food and land for growth. This is God bringing to pass His ultimate plan for His people. God can provide for His people anywhere, anytime, anyhow. It doesn't matter if they were in a foreign land; so long as God was involved, they flourished. You can get a Goshen in Egypt. You can get that breakthrough in the most unlikely place and with the most unlikely method.

Joseph saw his dreams come through as he became the saving grace for his family. You can never tell if you'll be the Joseph in your family; would you yield yourself to God for maximum impact? Would you let God reveal your life's path to you early? Until you see, you can't be—dream or Vision births fulfillment. But, if you can see, you can achieve. Every human is endowed with a unique ability to manifest; when you discover, develop, and use your abilities, you become a sharp threshing tool in the hand of God. I pray the Lord will help us fulfill His mandate in our lives in Jesus' name.

Chapter 13

JOSEPH'S FATHER RELEASES BLESSING.

Genesis 49

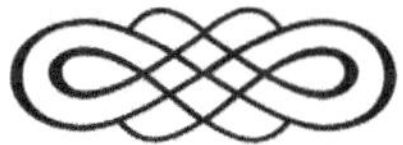

When you think of it, there are four fundamental questions of life. You've asked them, I've asked them, every thinking person asks them. They boil down to this; origin, meaning, morality, and destiny. 'How did I come into being? What brings life meaning? How do I know right from wrong? Where am I headed after I die?' **Ravi Zacharias**

Across customs and traditions, fathers blessing their children before they die seemed familiar at that time. So, it was in the days of the Bible. The book of Genesis emphasizes a father's blessing to his sons. In Jacob's case, Abraham, Isaac, and Jacob all formally blessed their offspring and some of their grandchildren. It was a great honor to have a father's blessing; losing one was to suffer a curse.

A father's blessing to his sons in the Old Testament featured encouragement, information about each son's inheritance, and prognostications about the future. For instance, Isaac's blessing on Jacob (intended for Esau) granted him control over his sibling and access to the earth's abundance (Genesis 27:28-29). As with God's promise to Abraham, it also stated that people who blessed Jacob would be blessed, while those who cursed him would be condemned.

In dismay, Esau questioned, "Have you not prepared a blessing for me?" after learning that Jacob had tricked his father and taken the blessing intended for him in Genesis 27:36. Isaac told him that he was superior to him. Still, he also foretold that Esau would take one day to rebel against Jacob's leadership (verses 39-40).

In this section, we shall look at how God blesses his children through their earthly fathers, how a curse from a father stands and is confirmed by God as well, and talk about how careful we should be with our character.

God Blesses His Children through their Earthly Fathers

When Jacob was to die, he sent for his children. First, he blessed Manasseh and Ephraim before contacting the other children. Some got blessed, while others got cursed. Why is it so? Let's find out.

Jacob foretold their destiny when he blessed his twelve sons (Genesis 49). Many of these prophecies were directly fulfilled in the Bible, demonstrating the miraculous ability granted to Jacob as the patriarch of the twelve tribes. "Judah, your brothers shall praise you;

your hand shall be upon the neck of your foes; your father's sons shall fall before you," Jacob declared in one of his blessings (Genesis 49:8). The blessing also foretold that Judah would produce monarchs and that one King would ultimately command "the obedience of the nations" (verse 10). Later, the descendants of Judah were the tribe from which King David descended and whose territory Jerusalem was situated. Finally, the tribe of Judah would be where Jesus Christ would originate (Matthew 1:3).

Jacob's comments to Issachar provide yet another instance of a miraculous prophecy: "He saw that a resting place was good and that the land was pleasant" (Genesis 49:15). Later, lower Galilee, including the Valley of Jezreel, which included lush, fruitful farmland, would be inherited by Issachar's descendants. Benjamin is a hungry wolf, eating victims in the morning and splitting the take in the evening, according to a prophecy that was given to Jacob's youngest son (Genesis 49:27). Benjamin's tribe would produce numerous military leaders in Israel, such as Ehud, King Saul, and Saul's son Jonathan, displaying a robust, combative character (Judges 5:14; 20:16; 1 Chronicles 8:40; 2 Chronicles 14:8; 17:17).

Now let's find out why some were not blessed at all; instead got a curse.

The Pronouncement on Reuben, Simeon, and Levi vs. the Rest

Jacob was so sure of what he was about to tell his children. Hence, he said: "Gather yourself together to me, so I tell you what will befall each of you later in life" (Gen 49:1).

Now let's take a look at the pronouncement on Reuben and Simeon.

"Reuben, thou art my firstborn, my might, and the beginning of my strength, the Excellency of dignity, and the Excellency of power: unstable as water, thou shall not excel; because thou went up to thy father's bed; then defiled thou it: he went up to my couch. Simeon and Levi are brethren; instruments of cruelty are in their habitations. O my soul, come not thou into their secret; unto their assembly, mine honor, be not thou united: in their anger, they slew a man, and in their self-will, they dug down a wall. Cursed be their anger, for it was fierce; and their wrath, for it was cruel: I will divide them between Jacob, and scatter them in Israel." Genesis 49:3-7

The opening sentence of Jacob was somewhat harsh but the reality. Reuben, my firstborn, my might, my early strength, you're supposedly my pride; but unstable as water. The following statement is mind-blowing; "you shall not prosper" why? Because you slept with my wife! Wow, that wasn't good. Reuben thought Jacob had forgiven him since he had said nothing about it since the incident happened, but he was wrong. Jacob had been waiting for a day like this. What a bomb Jacob released!

Simeon got a curse because of uncontrolled anger. These two guys were the only ones that got a curse from Jacob instead of a blessing. And the reasons are clear; I want to emphasize this. Why should I get a curse instead of a gift? I implore you to go to the previous page and read the blessings of Benjamin, Judah, and the rest again. God was releasing his blessings through Jacob to his children.

Be Mindful of what you do with your Youthful Life.

The law of cause and effect is authentic. The law of sowing and reaping is also fundamental. Whatever a man plants, that's precisely what he will reap.

Attitudes can be seeds; every man's action is a seed, and you plant them as you exhibit those characteristics daily. And remember, they'll produce results someday. If you let your flesh dictate your actions, you'll reap its produce later in life; if you allow anger to push you, you'll reap its fruits later on; if you let youthful lust drive you, you'll reap its fruits later on.

What you do doesn't matter; you'll get a reward someday. The question is, what are you doing with your youthful life now? How are you living your life? Reuben never knew what he did when he was a youth would return to hurt him several years later. So what are you doing now that could jeopardize your future? Check your actions, and be sure you're not piling up negative results for tomorrow.

CONCLUSION

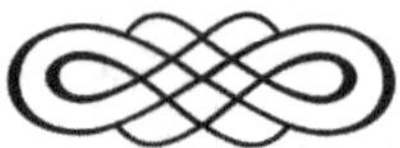

Joseph's life is exemplary; it is extraordinary that every parent would love to see their children replicate or possibly surpass. Young ones in our generation also aspire to replicate that fit in their generation. Churches and other Christian organizations desire to see their youths manifest Joseph's grace: the grace to discover purpose early in life and stick to it until absolute fulfillment. This is why you see many church programs with the theme: "The Josephs of Our Time," "A Joseph in the Making," "The Joseph in You," and so many attractive and exciting captions like that. But the question is, are we ready to journey through the terrain Joseph traveled through? Those terrains were rugged, you know!

Joseph didn't just emerge overnight. He took a long compulsory journey to destiny, a trip that shaped and made him fit for the glory. Specific catalysts necessitated his attainment of the credit; they included abstinence, having promising dreams/visions, keeping focus, absolute obedience to God and your Godly parents, and personal drive for more. What dream do you have at age 17, 23, 25, or 30? Unfortunately, many of us don't even know why we exist, yet we want to be like Joseph; how's that possible?

Yes, I agree you desire to be like Joseph, but do you think there'll be opposition? Are you aware that every enviable destiny attracts both good and evil? Or do you think it's everyone that celebrates you? Don't you know that there are star hunters everywhere? Pharaoh hunted Moses' destiny, and Herod did the same when Jesus was born; what makes you think the devil will not come after you when he discovers you're a threat to his kingdom? Beware of satanic star hunters, destiny killers, and dream "aborters." Joseph suffered this at the hands of his brother, not even an outsider. It wasn't a funny experience, as we know all that transpired.

In life's journey, you'll get to a point where challenges will set in, a dark junction where it looks like your dreams aren't coming through. That was Joseph's life in Potiphar's house, sold into slavery and bondage, but God was with him. Can you say aloud to yourself; God's with me! God never leaves us to face seasons alone; He's always available to help. His presence with Joseph made all the difference in Potiphar's house. If there's anything you should not lose at any time, it is the PRESENCE of God.

Whenever God's set to launch a man to a higher level, He takes him through some tests; the test of integrity, pride, and purity. Joseph passed all three tests; will you pass your own? Music minister, are you still working on your backups? Mr. Instrumentalist, are you not becoming too high-minded that the music director can't talk to you again? Beloved, God is counting on us to raise the banner of purity so high in our generation; will heaven be proud of you?

Deciding to maintain purity, honesty, and humility comes with a price. Joseph fought hard, even putting his life on the line to keep his stand for God. But, of course, the action landed him in prison. How resolved are you to maintain your stand for God? Do you easily give in to satanic pressures? Think about it!

I want you to know that God will do anything if we are eager to give up anything. In prison, He prospered Joseph. Joseph remained spiritually relevant and alert. His willingness to interpret other people's dreams eventually paid off as he got divinely lifted from prison to the palace. Stay relevant even in the jail of lack and challenges; God is with you.

One of the marks of greatness is the ability to forgive and move on quickly. Joseph did not dwell in the past; he forgave his master's wife, forgave his brothers, and moved on. It could be challenging to do this sometimes, especially when you have a scenario like that of Joseph and his brothers. Still, God expects you to forgive all the same. Joseph eventually became a generational deliverer, just like he dreamt when he was only 17 years old; his dreams finally saw the light. His family enjoyed his influence in Egypt as they were given a pleasant land to settle in. His father blessed him while some others got a course when Jacob was to die. He became the most sought-after; is that the kind of life you genuinely admire or aspire to have?

God is still searching for the generational deliverers of our time; will you make yourself available and useable? It's a fact that some of us genuinely crave higher levels, but can God trust you? Can God be bold to tell the devil, see my daughter, see my son, and look at how faithful they are to me…....? This is the main issue; the ability to walk with all through life's journey, live in the consciousness of His presence, and please Him even in pain.

God has his remnants in every generation. In lesson 01 on the Life of Joseph, as presented back in 2009, the story of Joseph is compared to that of Daniel. Look at this beautiful narrative on this.

The one stands at the commencement, the other at the end of the Jewish history of revelation; they were both representatives of the true God and his people at heathen courts; both were exemplary in their pure walk before the Lord; both were endowed with the gift of bringing into clear light the dim presentiments of truth which express themselves among the heathen in Godsent dreams; both were gifted with great wisdom and insight, and for this reason highly honored among the nations (C. A. Auberlen, quoted in Taylor, 223).[6]

In the same way, you can follow the story of Joseph and others like Daniel, whom God used in different generations to serve him in the best way possible; God is waiting on you to obey him at your age, and it remains a testimony to other generations to come. Therefore, I pray that you will leave a legacy in this world even as you one day transition to the next. In my first book 'Stand Out and Be Counted' I wrote chapter 12 on the subject, 'Build Your Legacy' You may want to read this chapter that discusses how best you can build your legacy for posterity.[7]

---

[6] Mount Calvary Baptist Church Greenville SC, "The Life of Joseph: Lesson 1 - Introduction," 2009, 6.

[7] Rev. Paul Ekal Lokol, *Stand Out and Be Counted: How to Activate and Unlock Your Full Potential for the Benefit of Your next Generation*, 1st ed. (Nairobi - Kenya: Bafeafrica Inspiration Networks, 2017), 102–108.

Yes, Joseph journeyed from slavery to prime minister; are you ready to set out and pursue your destiny with all it takes? **YES, YOU CAN BY THE GRACE OF GOD.**

REFERENCES

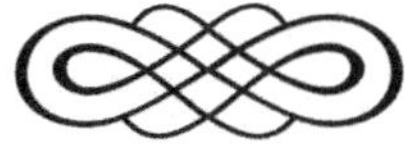

Baptist Church Greenville SC, Mount Calvary. "The Life of Joseph: Lesson 1 - Introduction," 2009.

Brill, Leiden E.J. *A Study of the Biblical Story of Joseph (Genesis 37 - 50)*. Vol. XX. Netherlands, 1970.

Calvine, Brenda. "Behind Every Glory There a Is a Story." *Behind Every Glory, There Is a Story*, 2015. http://brendacalvince.blogspot.com/2015/01/behind-every-glory-there-is-story.html.

Ekal Lokol, Rev. Paul. *Stand Out and Be Counted: How to Activate and Unlock Your Full Potential for the Benefit of Your next Generation*. 1st ed. Nairobi - Kenya: Bafeafrica Inspiration Networks, 2017.

Erickson, Matt. *The Life of Joseph: God's Sovereignty in Our Suffering*. A Lenten Devotional. Eastbrook Church, n.d. www.eastbrook.org.

International, Amazing Facts. "Devotional: Joseph, Master of Dreams: Lesson 11," June 11, 2022. Accessed February 4, 2023. https://www.amazingfacts.org/media-library/media/e/26730/t/joseph--master-of-dreams.

Jacob, Pastor. *Joseph and the Gospel of Many Colors*, 2014. www.martinsburgchurch.org/joseph.

Reid, Ainsley. *Biblical Principles of Building Wealth.* AR Book Publishing, 2020.

Profiles of Faith: Joseph - Faithfulness Brings Blessing. https://www.ucg.org/the-good-news/profiles-of-faith-joseph-faithfulness-brings-blessing

Sen, Rajib. "Brilliance Certified by Mensa." Alive, no. 395, Delhi Press, Sept. 2015, p. 35.

The 35+ Think Positively Quotes Page 9 - ↑QUOTLR↑. https://quotlr.com/quotes-about-think-positively/9

Ready to Give Up on Crate Training? Try These Tips! https://www.redstonevet.com/services/dogs/blog/ready-give-crate-training-try-these-tips

Law of sowing and reaping – The National. https://www.thenational.com.pg/law-of-sowing-and-reaping/